Internet Research

ILLUSTRATED, Sixth Edition

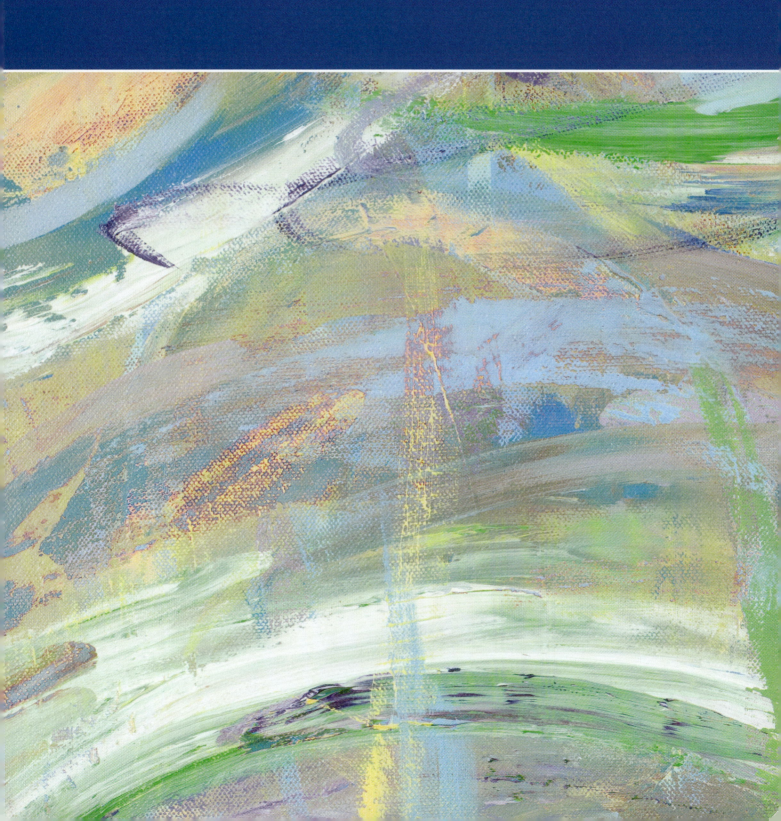

Internet Research

ILLUSTRATED, Sixth Edition

Barker • Barker • Pinard

COURSE TECHNOLOGY
CENGAGE Learning

Australia • Brazil • Japan • Korea • Mexico • Singapore • Spain • United Kingdom • United States

COURSE TECHNOLOGY
CENGAGE Learning·

Internet Research—Illustrated, Sixth Edition
Donald I. Barker, Melissa S. Barker, Katherine T. Pinard

Executive Editor: Marjorie Hunt

Associate Acquisitions Editor: Amanda Lyons

Senior Product Manager: Christina Kling-Garrett

Associate Product Manager: Kim Klasner

Editorial Assistant: Brandelynn Perry

Director of Marketing: Elisa Roberts

Developmental Editor: Kim Crowley

Content Project Manager: Heather Hopkins

Permission Specialist: Kathleen Ryan

QA Manuscript Reviewers: John Frietas, Jeff Schwartz, Susan Whalen

Cover Designer: GEX Publishing Services

Cover Artist: Mark Hunt

Composition: GEX Publishing Services

Copyeditor: Mark Goodin

Proofreader: Harold Johnson

Indexer: Elizabeth Cunningham

For product information and technology assistance, contact us at
Cengage Learning Customer & Sales Support, 1-800-354-9706

For permission to use material from this text or product, submit all requests online at **ceng age.com/permissions**
Further permissions questions can be emailed to
permissionrequest@cengage.com

Library of Congress Control Number: 2011939364

ISBN-13: 978-1-133-19038-7

ISBN-10: 1-133-19038-3

Course Technology
20 Channel Center Street
Boston, Massachusetts 02210
USA

Cengage Learning is a leading provider of customized learning solutions with office locations around the globe, including Singapore, the United Kingdom, Australia, Mexico, Brazil, and Japan. Locate your local office at:
international.cengage.com/region

Cengage Learning products are represented in Canada by Nelson Education, Ltd.

To learn more about Course Technology, visit **www.cengage.com/coursetechnology**

To learn more about Cengage Learning, visit **www.cengage.com**

Purchase any of our products at your local college store or at our preferred online store **www.cengagebrain.com**

Printed in China
2 3 4 5 6 7 17 16 15 14 13 12

Brief Contents

Contents

Preface

Welcome to *Internet Research—Illustrated, Sixth Edition*. If this is your first experience with the Illustrated series, you'll see that this book has a unique design: each skill is presented on two facing pages, with steps on the left and screens on the right. The layout makes it easy to learn a skill without having to read a lot of text and flip pages to see an illustration.

This book is an ideal learning tool for a wide range of learners—the "rookies" will find the clean design easy to follow and focused with only essential information presented, and the "hotshots" will appreciate being able to move quickly through the lessons to find the information they need without reading a lot of text. The design also makes this a great reference after the course is over! See the illustration on the right to learn more about the pedagogical and design elements of a typical lesson.

- Vastly expanded coverage of social media search, with an entire unit now dedicated to the topic.

- Explores how to use social media meta search engines to find information from multiple social media sites simultaneously.

- Additional emphasis on evaluating the value, veracity, and reliability of content found online.

- Continued attention to Boolean search and the use of other advanced search operators to maximize the efficacy of Internet research.

- Streamlined coverage of specialty searches and the use of subject directories, using state-of-the-art search techniques.

- Lesson steps in this new edition provide instructions for accessing specific sites; there is no longer a need to use an online companion to complete the steps.

Each two-page spread focuses on a single skill.

An introduction briefly explains why the lesson skill is important.

A case scenario motivates the steps and puts learning in context.

UNIT D
Internet Research

Navigating the Blogosphere

The **blogosphere** is made up of all blogs and their interconnections. The blogosphere continues to grow, in large part due to sites that allow people to create blogs for free, such as Google's Blogger, which has over 70 million estimated unique monthly visitors. You can search for information on individual blog sites, but, fortunately, blog search engines have evolved to help people quickly and efficiently locate specific information in the blogosphere. Table D-2 describes some of the popular blog search engines. To help you find more information and experts about biomass as a renewable energy, Bob suggests you search the blogosphere to find other informed opinions on this subject.

STEPS

1. **Type technorati.com in your browser's Address bar, then press [Enter]**
   The Technorati home page appears. Note that the top of the page contains a variety of categories you can click to view popular blogs in each category. The page also includes a Search text box, and to the left of the Search text box are the Blogs and Posts buttons. These buttons allow you to specify whether you want the search to return blog titles or posts. Since you want to find experts in biomass as a renewable energy, you decide to search blogs in hopes of finding bloggers with this specialized knowledge.

2. **Click the Blogs button in the Search text box, type biomass renewable energy in the Search text box, then click the Search button**
   The search results appear, similar to those shown in Figure D-7. For each result, the blog title, blog URL, the title of a recent post, and a brief description of that post appears. An Authority rating is also given for each result as denoted by the number in the "Auth:" column to the right of each result. Technorati Authority uses a proprietary algorithm to evaluate and rank a blog's standing and influence in the blogosphere on a scale from 0 to 1,000. The higher the Authority number, the better.

   QUICK TIP
   You can click the page numbers at the top and bottom of the search results to see additional search returns.

3. **Scroll through the results, and click the title of a blog that appears relevant to your needs and that has a high Authority rating**
   A description of the blog appears. Scan the blog description to determine if it appears to belong to an expert in biomass as a renewable energy. You could click the URL to go directly to the blog. However, for now, you decide to explore further by refining your search using Technorati's advanced search features.

4. **Click your browser's Back button, then click the Click to refine this search link**
   The Refine options page appears. Here you can choose to change whether blog titles or posts are returned. You can also choose whether to search in blogs, on news sites, or both (the "all" option). In addition, you can restrict your search by topic and Authority rating. Finally, you can order search results by relevance (the default) or date. To narrow your search to experts dedicated to "green" energy sources, you decide to refine your search by category.

5. **Click the Filter by list arrow, click Green, then click the Refine this search button**
   The search results are refreshed, showing just the blogs in the green category. Notice that you have significantly reduced the number of blogs to examine.

6. **Click a blog title that appears relevant to your needs and that has a high Authority rating, read the blog description, then click the blog's URL to navigate to the blog's site**
   The blog appears in your browser window with the most recent post at the top. To confirm the Authority rating for yourself, you want to find out about the blogger's credentials. Most bloggers post information about themselves on an About Me page.

7. **Click the About Me link (or something similar), then read the blog author's description of him or herself**
   Finally, you should read a few blog posts so you can determine if the blog content suits your needs.

8. **Read the first few posts in the blog**

Internet Research 88   Searching the Social Web

Tips and troubleshooting advice are located right where you need them—next to the step itself.

Large screen shots keep
students on track as
they complete steps.

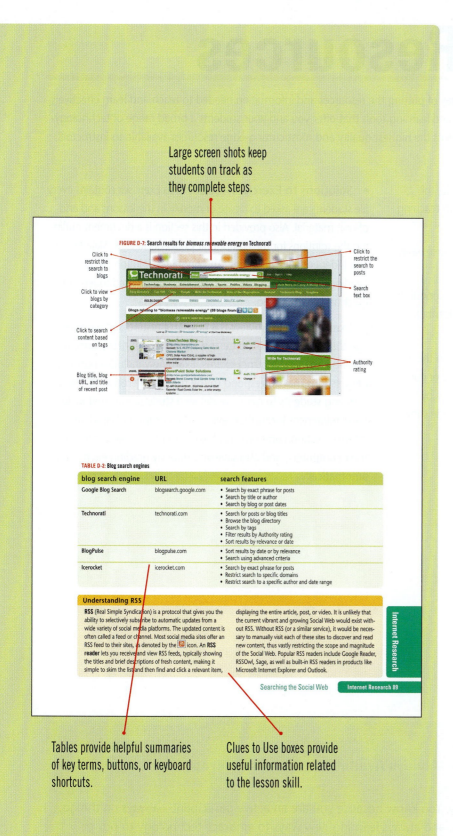

Tables provide helpful summaries
of key terms, buttons, or keyboard
shortcuts.

Clues to Use boxes provide
useful information related
to the lesson skill.

Assignments

The assignments on the yellow pages at the
end of each unit increase in difficulty.
Additional case studies provide a variety of
interesting and relevant exercises for students
to practice skills. Assignments include:

- The **Concepts Review** consists of multiple
  choice, matching, and screen identifica-
  tion questions.

- The **Skills Review** provides additional
  hands-on, step-by-step reinforcement.

- The **Independent Challenges** are case
  projects requiring critical thinking and
  application of the unit skills. Independent
  Challenges increase in difficulty, with the
  first one in each unit being the easiest.
  Independent Challenges 2 and 3 become
  increasingly open-ended, requiring more
  independent problem solving.

- The **Real Life Independent Challenges**
  are practical exercises to help students
  with their everyday lives.

- The **Advanced Challenge Exercises (ACE)**
  are set within the Independent Challenges
  to provide optional steps for more
  advanced students.

- The **Visual Workshops** are practical, self-
  graded capstone projects that require
  independent problem solving.

Internet Research Sites Appendix

New Internet Research Sites Appendix contains names and URLs of Web sites, grouped
by category, you can use to perform different
types of research on the Internet.

Instructor Resources

The Instructor Resources CD is Course Technology's way of putting the resources and information needed to teach and learn effectively into your hands. With an integrated array of teaching and learning tools that offer you and your students a broad range of technology-based instructional options, we believe this CD represents the highest quality and most cutting-edge resources available to instructors today. The resources available with this book are:

• **Instructor's Manual**—Available as an electronic file, the Instructor's Manual includes detailed lecture topics with teaching tips for each unit.

• **Sample Syllabus**—Prepare and customize your course easily using this sample course outline.

• **PowerPoint Presentations**—Each unit has a corresponding PowerPoint presentation that you can use in lecture, distribute to your students, or customize to suit your course.

• **Figure Files**—The figures in the text are provided on the Instructor Resources CD to help you illustrate key topics or concepts. You can create traditional overhead transparencies by printing the figure files. Or, you can create electronic slide shows by using the figures in a presentation program such as PowerPoint.

• **Solutions to Exercises**—Solutions to Exercises contains every file students are asked to create or modify in the lessons and end-of-unit material. Also provided in this section is a document outlining the solutions for the end-of-unit Concepts Review, Skills Review, and Independent Challenges. An Annotated Solution File and Grading Rubric accompany each file and can be used together for quick and easy grading.

• **ExamView**—ExamView is a powerful testing software package that allows you to create and administer printed, computer (LAN-based), and Internet exams. ExamView includes hundreds of questions that correspond to the topics covered in this text, enabling students to generate detailed study guides that include page references for further review. The computer-based and Internet testing components allow students to take exams at their computers, and also save you time by grading each exam automatically.

COURSECASTS **Learning on the Go. Always Available...Always Relevant.**

Our fast-paced world is driven by technology. You know because you are an active participant—always on the go, always keeping up with technological trends, and always learning new ways to embrace technology to power your life. Let CourseCasts, hosted by Ken Baldauf of Florida State University, be your guide to weekly updates in this ever-changing space. These timely, relevant podcasts are produced weekly and are available for download at *http://coursecasts.course.com* or directly from iTunes (search by CourseCasts). CourseCasts are a perfect solution to getting students (and even instructors) to learn on the go!

Figure Credits

Unit A

Figures A-7, A-8, A-9, A-10 Courtesy of © 2011 Google

Figures A-11, A-13 Courtesy of © 2011 Microsoft Corporation

Figure A-14 Courtesy of © 2011 Google

Figure A-15 Courtesy of © 2011 Google and © Carbonfund.org Copyright 2003–2011

Figure A-16 Courtesy of © 2011 Google

Figure A-18 Courtesy of The Environmental and Energy Study Institute (eesi.org)

Figure A-19 Courtesy of © People & the Planet 2000–2010

Figure A-22 Courtesy of Gawker Media

Figure A-23, Courtesy of © 2011 Google

Figure A-24, Courtesy of © 2011 epa.gov

Unit B

Figures B-3, B-5, B-7, B-11, B-13, B-14, B-15, B-16 Courtesy of © 2011 Google

Figure B-16 Courtesy of © 2011 InfoSpace, Inc. All Rights Reserved

Figure B-17 Courtesy of © 2009–2011 Yippy, Inc.

Figure B-22 Courtesy of NASA.gov

Unit C

Figures C-1, C-2 Open Directory Project courtesy of Copyright © 2011 Netscape

Figures C-3, C-4 Courtesy of Copyright 2011 Internet Scout Project - http://scout.wisc.edu

Figures C-6, C-7 Courtesy of © 2000–2011 Hot Neuron LLC. All Rights Reserved.

Figures C-8, C-9 Courtesy of © 2011 Google

Figures C-10, C-11 Courtesy of © 2009–2011 SuperMedia LLC. All rights reserved

Figure C-12 Courtesy of © Elsevier 2011

Figures C-13, C-14 Reproduced with permission from the ipl2 Consortium, copyright 2011 by the ipl2 Consortium (http://www.ipl.org). All rights reserved.

Figures C-15, C-16 Courtesy of USA.gov, the U.S. government's official web portal

Figure C-17 Courtesy of © 2000–2011 Hot Neuron LLC. All Rights Reserved.

Figure C-18 Open Directory Project courtesy of Copyright © 2011 Netscape

Unit D

Figure D-1 © 2011 EzineArticles.com All Rights Reserved Worldwide

Figure D-2 Courtesy of TagCrowd

Figure D-3 Courtesy of LinkedIn Corporation © 2011 with permission of Dr. Michael Brady

Figures D-4, D-5 Courtesy of LinkedIn Corporation © 2011

Figure D-6 Courtesy of © Technorati, Inc

Figure D-7 Courtesy of © 2011 Twitter

Figure D-8 Courtesy of © 2011 Twitter with permission of Dr. Maureen Griffin

Figure D-9 Courtesy of © 2011 Google

Figure D-10 Reproduced with permission of Yahoo! Inc. ©2011 Yahoo! Inc. YAHOO!, the YAHOO! logo, FLICKR, and the FLICKR logo are registered trademarks of Yahoo! Inc.

Figure D-11 Courtesy of © Digg Inc. 2011

Figure D-12 © 2011 EzineArticles.com All Rights Reserved Worldwide

Figures D-13, D-14 Copyright © 2011 Answers Corporation

Figures D-15, D-16 © Samepoint.com LLC.

Figure D-17 Courtesy of © Digg Inc. 2011

Figure D-18 Courtesy of Library of Congress

Acknowledgements

Donald I. Barker, **Melissa S. Barker**, and **Katherine T. Pinard**

Creating a book is a team effort. We sincerely thank our families and friends for their unfailing patience and generous support; Marjorie Hunt for publishing the book; Christina Kling Garrett for managing the project; Kathleen Ryan for gathering permissions; and our excellent developmental editor, Kim T. M. Crowley, for corrections and invaluable suggestions.

Read This Before You Begin

Frequently Asked Questions

What software was used to write and test this book?

This book was written and tested using a typical installation of Microsoft Windows 7.

The browsers used for any steps that require a browser are Internet Explorer 9 and Firefox 6.

Do I need to be connected to the Internet to complete the steps and exercises in this book?

All of the exercises in this book assume that your computer is connected to the Internet.

What do I do if my screen is different from the figures shown in this book?

This book was written and tested on computers with monitors set at a resolution of 1024 × 768. If your screen shows more or less information than the figures in the book, your monitor is probably set at a higher or lower resolution. If you don't see something on your screen, you might have to scroll down or up to see the object identified in the figures.

Searching the Internet Effectively

Files You Will Need:

No files needed.

Finding lots of irrelevant and potentially unreliable information on the Internet is easier than finding information you want and trust. In this unit, you learn about search tools, strategies, analysis, and Web page evaluation to maximize your chances of locating relevant reliable content that meets your needs, as well as learning how to cite your online sources in a standard format. You work in the city planning office in Portland, Oregon. The city is working toward becoming more energy independent, and you are to create a list of Web resources on alternative energy. Although you use the Web, you realize your skills need some polishing to do a quality job. You ask your friend, Bob Johnson, a reference librarian at a Portland University reference library, to help you learn the basics of Internet searching.

OBJECTIVES

Understand Internet search tools

Create an Internet research strategy

Identify the right keywords

Perform a basic search

Add keywords

Use phrase searching

Analyze search results

Understand evaluative criteria

Evaluate a Web page

Cite online resources

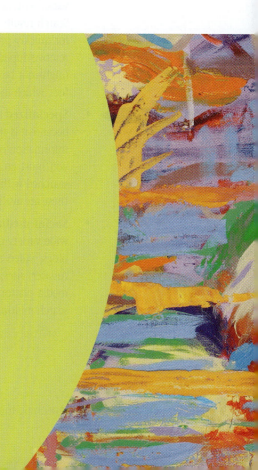

Understanding Internet Search Tools

The **World Wide Web** is an enormous repository of information stored on millions of computers all over the world. The **Internet** is a vast global network of interconnected smaller networks. You use the Internet to connect to information on the Web. You use **Internet search tools**, services that locate information on the Web, to find the information you need. Your **search query** tells the search tool specifically what information you want. Search tools can be divided into four major categories: search engines, metasearch engines, specialized search engines, and social media search engines. Different search tools are better for finding different types of information, and no tool searches the entire Internet. Figure A-1 illustrates the four types of search tools and the areas of the Web they cover.  Before you start your search for Web pages about alternative energy, Bob gives you a brief overview of search tools.

DETAILS

Types of search tools include the following:

- **Search engines** enable you to locate Web pages that contain keywords you enter in a search form. **Keywords** are the nouns and verbs, and sometimes important adjectives, that describe the major concepts of your search topic. A program called a **spider** crawls or scans the Web to index the keywords in Web pages. The indexes, or indices, created by spiders match the keywords you enter in a search engine and return a list of links to Web pages that contain these keywords. Because this is a precise process, it provides a narrow search of the Web and works well for finding specific content. Because spiders take months to index even a small portion of the Web, search engine results are limited, and some might be out of date. No single search engine covers the entire Web, so consider using more than one engine for important searches. To find out more about search engines, visit SearchEngineWatch.com or SearchEngineShowdown.com.

- **Metasearch engines** offer a single search form to query multiple search engines simultaneously. As with search engines, you enter keywords to retrieve links to Web pages that contain matching information. Search results are compiled from other search engines, rather than from the Web. Metasearches are useful for quickly providing the highest-ranked results from multiple search engines. Better metasearch engines remove duplicate results and rank the results based on relevancy to your query. Unfortunately, these results might not be optimal; the best search engines are often excluded from a metasearch because they charge fees, which metasearch engine providers decline to pay.

QUICK TIP

Major search engines constantly work toward being able to search parts of the Web that are currently invisible to their spiders.

- **Specialized search engines** allow you to find information that is "invisible" to traditional search engines because it is stored in proprietary databases, specialty directories, or reference sites. The vast majority of the information on the Web is in this invisible area, usually called the **deep Web**. To retrieve this information, you must go to a specific site and use its unique search interface. Although many of these sites can be searched with specialized search engines, others require a subscription or charge a fee for access. Many of these are available at libraries.

- **Social media search engines** offer the means to find content created by the masses and experts on a wide variety of social media platforms. **Social media platforms** include social networks, blogs, micro-blogs, video and photo sharing sites, social news sites and article directories, and Q&A (Question-and-Answer) sites, as well as bookmarking sites and news aggregators. Finding relevant information on social media platforms can be a challenge. Social media search engines have evolved to provide the means to search multiple social media sites simultaneously.

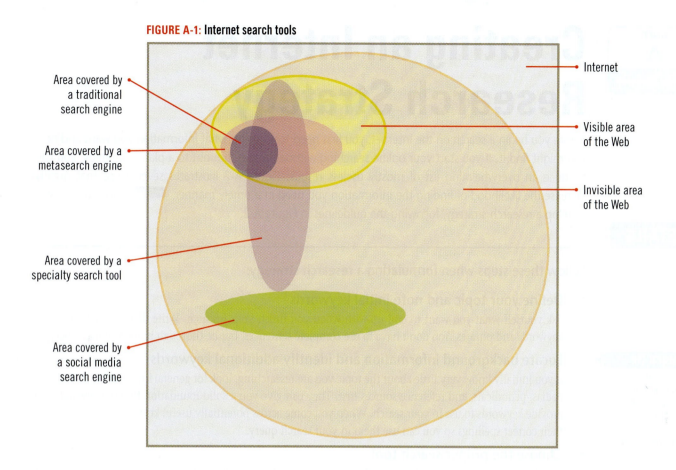

Area covered by
a traditional
search engine

Area covered by a
metasearch engine

Area covered by a
specialty search tool

Area covered by
a social media
search engine

Internet

Visible area
of the Web

Invisible area
of the Web

Using a search toolbar

Google, Microsoft, and Yahoo! provide search toolbars that enable you to search the Internet from your desktop or browser, without actually visiting the search engines. Each toolbar is closely tied to its parent search engine, and they share many features such as the ability to block pop-ups, automatically complete forms, and protect against spyware. The Google toolbar checks the spelling of your queries, translates English words into other languages, and blocks pop-ups. The

Bing toolbar provides buttons that when you point to them, display the current page on various popular sites, such as Facebook, or get current weather or stock information. The Yahoo! toolbar provides one-click access to features on its site, such as Yahoo! Mail, weather, and news. (You download these search toolbars from their respective company Web sites. Just search the sites using the toolbar name.)

Internet Research

Creating an Internet Research Strategy

Before you begin a search on the Internet, you first need to focus on what information you want and how you might find it. If you start your online searching without giving thought to a plan or strategy, you can produce an overwhelming list of mostly useless results. Figure A-2 illustrates seven steps that greatly increase the likelihood of finding the information you need in a timely manner.  Bob suggests you develop a research strategy, following the guidelines in Figure A-2.

DETAILS

Follow these steps when formulating a research strategy:

- **Define your topic and note initial keywords**

    Ask yourself what you want to end up with when you finish your research. Write down your topic. Note keywords and phrases. You don't have to use complete sentences, but be thorough in identifying concepts.

QUICK TIP

If you get stuck at any point in your research, consult your local reference librarians. They are information experts.

- **Locate background information and identify additional keywords**

    If you initially know very little about the topic you are researching, look for general information in encyclopedias, periodicals, and reference sources first. They can give you a solid foundation for your research and provide keywords to use in your search. When you come across potentially useful keywords, note them and their correct spellings so you can use them in your search query.

- **Choose the proper search tool**

    Use the search tools that are best suited to retrieving the type of information you want to find. Table A-1 lists the most common search tools and provides information on how to select the best tool for your research needs. If you want specific content, search engines or metasearch engines are appropriate. When seeking information not normally tracked by these tools, turn to specialized search engines. When informed opinions or reviews and comments by the masses are useful, as in product evaluations, social media search engines are required. Combining these search tools provides the most thorough approach.

- **Translate your question into an effective search query**

    The first step in translating a question into an effective search query—which consists of a word, words, phrases, and symbols that a search engine can interpret—is to identify the keywords that best describe the topic. You use keywords to query either search engines or metasearch engines. You can also combine keywords with search operators and parentheses to construct complex searches for even more accuracy.

- **Perform your search**

    Search engines offer a variety of different search forms that contain fields in which you enter information specific to your search. The information you provide is used to return **search results**.

QUICK TIP

Understanding digital literacy is a lifelong skill and will be relevant in every career.

- **Evaluate your search results**

    The quantity and quality of results vary from one search engine to another. To ascertain the value of the information you find, you need to evaluate your search results, through identifying who authored the Web page or determining how current the information is.

- **Refine your search, if needed**

    If the quality or quantity of results is not what you need, return to an earlier step in the process to refine your strategy. Use what you learned from your first pass through this process to refine your search. First, try fine-tuning your search query, and then try a different search tool. If you are still not satisfied with your results, you might need to reevaluate your keywords. Perhaps they are too specific or obscure. If you are unable to do this or it isn't successful, you might need to seek more basic information on your topic. Or, rethink the topic—you might find that redefining it, based on what you have seen in your searches, would be helpful.

FIGURE A-2: Developing a research strategy

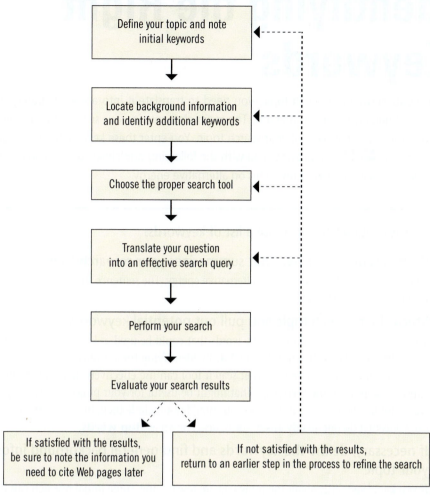

TABLE A-1: Common search tools

search tool	best for	where it searches	how to search	sample information	sample tools
Search engines	General or specific	Searches its own indexes that a re compiled from data gathered from the Web	Enter keywords, phrases, or complex search criteria	Alternative energy or solar panels	Google Yahoo! Bing
Metasearch engines	General or specific	Searches the indexes of multiple search engines simultaneously	Enter keywords, phrases, or complex search criteria	Alternative energy or solar panels	Startpage Yippy MetaCrawler
Specialized tools	More specific	Searches its own files or databases, directories, reference sites, government information, media, and search engines	Enter search term and browse directories	Latest news on solar panels	USA.gov SuperPages MagPortal
Social media search engines	More specific	Searches social media sites	Enter keywords, phrases, or complex search criteria, as well as browse directories	Opinions, reviews, and expert advice on solar panels	SocialMention Samepoint Topsy

Searching the Internet Effectively

Identifying the Right Keywords

After identifying your research topic, you need to translate it into a search strategy that optimizes your chances of finding useful information. The main elements in your search strategy are the keywords that describe the major concepts of your search topic. You enter these keywords into the search tool to return useful results. Bob provides you with the following guidelines to help you create a list of keywords to use in your search for Web resources on alternative energy.

DETAILS

Follow these guidelines to create a list of keywords:

- **Write a sentence or two that summarizes your research topic**

  You want to find Web resources on alternative energy. The sentence shown in Figure A-3 demonstrates how to state your research topic.

- **Study the research topic and pull out potential keywords**

  You look at this topic and decide the words that could be used as keywords are *alternative* and *energy*. You circle these words, as shown in Figure A-4. By identifying these words, you are starting to turn your topic statement into terms that an Internet search tool can use effectively. Remember, these are the words you expect to appear on the Web pages that might be useful for your project. Search engines normally do not search for the words *a*, *an*, and *the*, so you should not include them in most searches. See Table A-2 for typical words that do not qualify as keywords, also known as **stop words**.

- **If necessary, define the keywords and find general background information on your topic**

  If you know very little about the topic you are researching, some initial research can help you identify useful keywords. You look in a dictionary and see that *alternative energy* is energy from nonfossil fuels. It mentions solar and wind as examples. You then look in an encyclopedia to read a bit more about alternative energy. You find other types of alternative energies that might be useful, including water, biomass, and geothermal. Figure A-5 illustrates how to list the keywords you identified for your research topic.

QUICK TIP

Keep this list of keywords and related keywords handy, as you might find new words if you need to refine your search later using different search tools. Also, the words can help you identify topics in the pages you find.

- **Identify related terms using keyword generators**

  Keyword generators are tools that produce related keywords by using synonyms, plurals, misspellings, and other grammatical inflections. Web site designers use keyword generators to identify words that searchers will most likely use when trying to locate the content at a particular Web site. However, keyword generators can also be quite useful for searchers looking for the best possible keywords to find a topic. In addition to identifying related words to search on, keyword generators such as the Google AdWords Keyword Tool (which you can find at adwords.google.com) reveal the number of monthly searches using different variations of keywords. This can be useful because it indicates the keywords other people are using to find content. By using a keyword generator to expand your list of keywords, you help ensure that your queries are broad enough to find Web pages not indexed under the exact keywords in your initial list. Figure A-6 shows a list of related keywords generated by Google AdWords Keyword Tool.

TABLE A-2: Common words that are not useful in most searches

parts of speech	examples
Articles	a, an, the
Conjunctions and prepositions	and, or, but, in, of, for, on, into, from, than, at, to
Adjectives and adverbs	as, also, probably, however, very
Pronouns and verbs	this, that, these, those, is, be, see, do

FIGURE A-3: Write down your research topic statement

I want to find Web resources on alternative energy.

FIGURE A-4: Circle the keywords in your statement

I want to find Web resources on (alternative) (energy).

FIGURE A-5: Identify and list additional keywords

Keywords

alternative

energy

solar

wind

water

biomass

geothermal

FIGURE A-6: Identify synonyms and related words

Keywords	Synonyms & Related Terms
alternative	renewable, sustainable
energy	power
solar	panels, photovoltaic
wind	turbines, windmills
water	hydropower, hydroelectric
biomass	waste-to-energy, bioenergy
geothermal	heat, pumps

Performing a Basic Search

Search engines often differ in how they perform a basic search. It is always a good idea to view a search engine's Help page before you use it. An effective search statement at one search engine might not produce the best results at another. You can overcome these inconsistencies by using a trial-and-error approach to searching. At each search engine, try subtle variations on the search, changing your wording slightly. Note which search engines perform best for different kinds of searches.  You are ready to conduct a basic search using keywords you identified for alternative energy.

STEPS

1. **Start your Web browser, type google.com in the Address bar, then press [Enter]**
   The Google search form opens, as shown in Figure A-7.

TROUBLE
If a results page does not appear, Google Instant is not enabled on your computer. The results page will appear after you click the Search button.

2. **Click in the Search text box, then type s**
   A results page appears listing popular results that start with the letter *s*, and a list of suggested keywords appears below the Search text box. This feature is called Google Instant. As you type each additional character of your keywords, new results are returned. Also, Google Instant displays a guess as to the rest of the characters in the keywords in gray and displays results for that complete search phrase. You can click one of the suggested search terms, or you can finish typing your keywords.

3. **Type solar energy, then click the Search button** 🔍
   Your results should look similar to Figure A-8. Typically, the pages that best match the search query are listed first. However, be aware that many search engines accept payment for higher placement, so these sites are listed near the top where you typically expect the best matching results. Better search engines indicate this, sometimes with the word *Sponsored*. However, they are not required to disclose this. (You can visit the Search Engine Watch Web site at searchenginewatch.com for information about which engines accept sponsored placement.) The number of results you found will differ from the number shown in the figure.

4. **Delete your previous query in the Search text box, type solar power, then click** 🔍
   Notice that the browser displays a different number of results for this search than the last. One small change in a search query can radically change the number and quality of search results. Also, note that the number of results displayed often includes multiple pages per site; that is, your results might include several Web pages from the same Web site if each of those pages contains text that matches your search query. You know that using a different search tool can alter results, so you decide to try your search using Yahoo!.

5. **Click the Back button in your browser window**
   The search results for the first search you performed (for *solar energy*) again appear in the browser window.

6. **Open a new tab or browser window, type yahoo.com in the Address bar, then press [Enter]**
   The Yahoo! search form opens.

7. **Click in the Search text box, type solar energy, then click Web Search**
   Notice the number of results returned.

8. **Compare the number of results found for this search with the number of results found for the first search you performed in the first tab or browser window using Google**
   The number of results returned by each search engine differs, even though the search query was the same.

9. **In the tab or window containing the Google search results, click the Forward button**
   The results of your second search (for *solar power*) again appear in the window.

QUICK TIP
Most search tools allow either pressing [Enter] or clicking their search button to start a search.

10. **In the tab or window containing the Yahoo! search results, delete your previous query in the Search text box, type solar power, then press [Enter]**
    Notice again that the number of results for this search differs both from the previous search conducted in Yahoo! and from the number of results found for this search query in Google.

FIGURE A-7: Google search form

Links to other kinds of searches (Web is the default)

Search text box

Search button

Link to more information about Google

Search button that links you directly to Google's highest ranking result

Link to Google's privacy policy

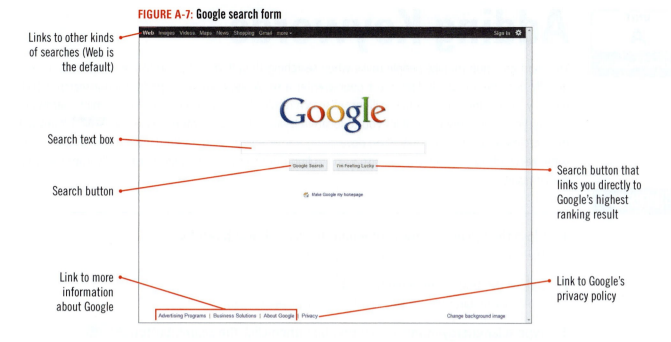

FIGURE A-8: Google search results

Your search query

Number of search results; yours will differ

Links to refine your search

Click the More search tools link to see more search options

Keywords highlighted in results

Search results

Click for advanced search options and other settings

Sponsored results

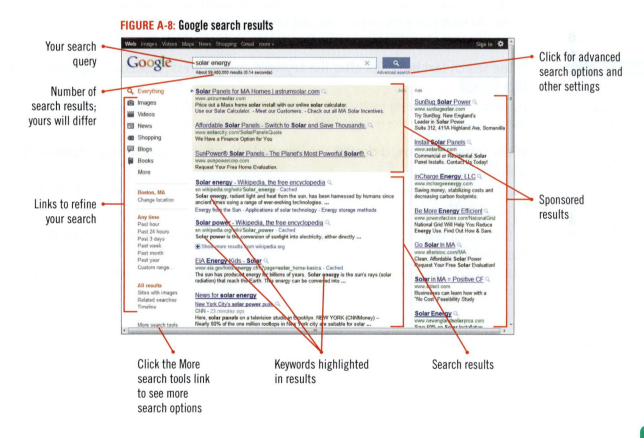

Why do search results vary with different search engines?

When a search engine spider scans the Internet for Web pages, it finds only a fraction of the Web pages that exist for any given topic. Each engine's spiders crawl different parts of the Web and a different scope of content. So when you use a different search engine, you are actually searching a slightly different part and a slightly different range of the Web. Also, each search engine uses different criteria to rank search results. So when your results are ranked for relevancy, different search engines might list similar results in a different order.

Adding Keywords

The most common mistake people make when searching the Internet is using too few keywords to adequately describe a topic. In fact, most people enter a single keyword when performing a search, which typically returns thousands, if not millions, of search results. Entering several keywords, which narrows or focuses your search results, enables you to locate relevant information more efficiently.  You want to locate more specific information on developing a solar energy plan for Portland, so you decide to add some keywords to your search. You also want to find out whether adding keywords really improves your search results.

STEPS

1. **Close the tab or window containing the Yahoo! search results**

   The tab containing the Google search results is the active tab.

2. **Delete the text in the Search text box**

   You decide to start with the basic search terms you used previously.

3. **Type solar energy in the Search text box, then click the Search button** 🔍

   On the page listing the search results, a count of the total results appears just below the Search text box. Because the number of results is quite large and the page descriptions are not particularly relevant to using solar energy as an alternative power source for a city, you decide to add the keyword *city* to your query.

> **QUICK TIP**
> Be creative and try variations in your searches, especially when using a search engine for the first time. You can discover a great deal about how the search engine functions by experimenting and then recording the number and quality of your results.

4. **In the Search text box, click after the keyword energy, press [Spacebar], type city, then click** 🔍

   This search returns far fewer results, as illustrated in Figure A-9. In addition, the page descriptions indicate that the information is more closely related to solar energy use in a city.

5. **In the Search text box, click after the keyword city, press [Spacebar], type develop, then click** 🔍

   Notice that the number of results is now even smaller and more closely related to how to develop solar energy for a city.

6. **In the Search text box, click after the keyword develop, press [Spacebar], type plan, then click** 🔍

   Your number of results is now even more limited and likely to be more relevant for your project. See Figure A-10.

FIGURE A-9: Search results narrowed by adding a keyword

Your original search phrase

Number of search results

Search results

Word added to the search phrase

Sponsored results

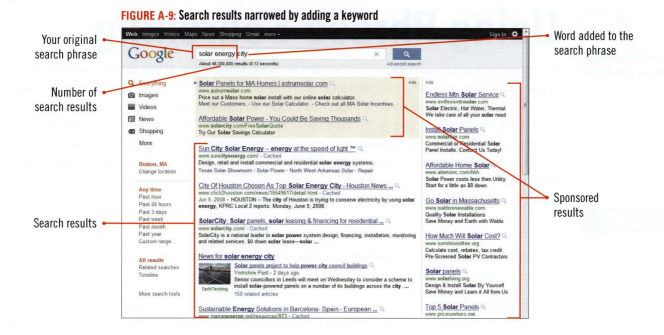

FIGURE A-10: Search results narrowed further

Your search query

Number of search results

Words added to the search phrase

Sponsored results

Search results

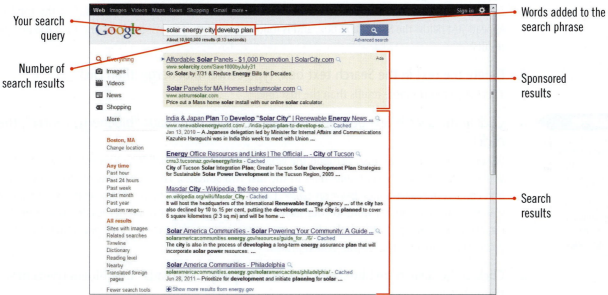

Arranging keywords

The order in which you place keywords in a search can be very important. Placing your most important keywords at the beginning of your search query causes a search engine to display results featuring the more important keywords at the top of your search results. For example, the keywords *hybrid electric vehicle* cause a search engine to first look for Web pages containing the word *hybrid*, then *electric*, and, finally, *vehicle*. Reversing the order of this search query (that is, *vehicle electric hybrid*) puts less emphasis on the keywords *hybrid* and *electric*, hence impacting the sequence of your search results. Depending on how the search engine finds results pages, it might also change the number of your search results.

Using Phrase Searching

When you construct a search with more than one keyword, you often need two or more words to be in a phrase rather than appearing independently on the results pages. For example, in the previous lesson, some of the results pages found were pages that happen to contain the words *solar* and *energy*, but they weren't actually about solar energy. To find these words in the correct order, you need to phrase search. In many search tools, **phrase searching** is accomplished by putting quotation marks ("") around the words you want to appear together in your results.  Bob suggests that your multikeyword searches can be refined even more with phrase searching. You want to have the most meaningful results returned, so you decide to try some phrase searches and compare the results.

STEPS

1. **Type bing.com in your browser's Address bar, then press [Enter]**
   The search form for Bing opens.

2. **Click in the Search text box**
   A list of trending searches on Bing (labeled POPULAR NOW) appears below the Search text box. **Trending searches** are current popular searches by others that use the keywords you typed or similar terms. If you conducted a search on Bing previously during your current session on the computer, the search terms you used appear above the trending searches.

3. **Type bioenergy center, then click the Search button 🔍**
   Figure A-11 illustrates the results for the search using these two keywords. A count of the total results appears just below the Search text box, and is followed by a list of sponsored links and then the first page of results.

4. **Delete the text in the Search text box, type center bioenergy, then click 🔍**
   This search returns more results than the first one.

> **QUICK TIP**
> Even though the phrase search returns far fewer results than the searches using two words, your first results might be the same, depending on how the search tool finds results pages.

5. **Click in the Search text box, edit the search query so it reads "bioenergy center", then click 🔍**
   Be sure to type quotation marks around the words *bioenergy center* to tell Bing to search for an exact phrase. You should now have fewer results than in the first two searches. This search has located only Web pages that contain the exact phrase *bioenergy center*. Figure A-12 compares the two-word searches with the phrase search. If you add another word to your search phrase, it will return even fewer results. You know the U.S. Department of Energy (DOE) funds a bioenergy center, and you want to find Web pages that discuss this, so you decide to include this in your search phrase.

6. **Click in the Search text box, edit the search query so it reads "doe bioenergy center", then click 🔍**
   See Figure A-13. The number of results is significantly reduced again because only Web pages that contain the phrase *DOE bioenergy center* are returned.

FIGURE A-11: Two-keyword search results in Bing

Your two-keyword search query

Number of results

Suggestions for related searches

Search results

FIGURE A-12: Comparing two-word searches with a phrase search

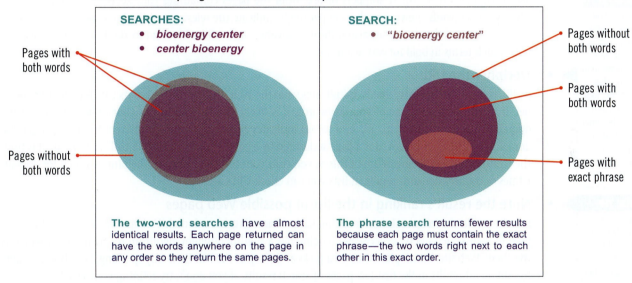

Pages with both words

Pages without both words

Pages without both words

Pages with both words

Pages with exact phrase

FIGURE A-13: Phrase search results in Bing

Your phrase search query

Number of results

Search results

Other ways to search using phrases

Most search engines allow phrase searching but not all in the same way. Most use quotation marks around words to indicate a phrase. However, some might automatically assume you are looking for a phrase when you enter two words in the Search text box, in which case quotation marks are redundant, but harmless. Some search engines might provide a drop-down menu or check box with an option for "exact phrase." Others might include an additional Search text box labeled "with this exact phrase." Sometimes the option for a phrase search might appear on an advanced search page. Use the Help or Search Tip pages at each search engine to learn how it uses and interprets phrase searching.

Analyzing Search Results

As you search, you need to scan the results pages to identify Web sites that seem most likely to be useful. Search results pages offer clues that can help you zero in on the best results. Knowing how to navigate and read the results page can save you time as you work with your search results. Figure A-14 identifies the key elements of a search results page. Bob has conducted a search using the search query *reduce "carbon footprint" "average american"*. He sits down with you to analyze the search results.

DETAILS

Use the following guidelines in determining the quality of search results:

QUICK TIP

As you search, you will become familiar with domain names. For academic information, look for .edu sites. For sites that sell or advocate, look for .com, .net, and .org. For professional or association sites, look for .pro. For government sites, look for .gov.

QUICK TIP

If you want to be taken directly to the one site Google thinks is the best, point to a suggestion in the list that appears below the Search text box, then click the I'm Feeling Lucky link to the right of the suggested search phrase.

- **Locate your search terms within the search result**
  Search engines often display snippets of text from the pages containing your keywords. The number of times your keywords show up in the snippet might indicate the relevance of the Web page to your search. The proximity of the words can also indicate relevance, as would a keyword in the URL. Google displays your search terms in bold for easy scanning.

- **Decipher the URL**
  A URL is often **mnemonic**; that is, it indicates what the Web site is about so that its URL is easier to remember. If the URL contains one of your keywords, it is likely to be mainly about your topic. The end of the domain name (.com, .edu, .jp, .uk, and so on) indicates either a certain type of Web site or its geographic domain. If a URL ends in .gov, it is a page sponsored by a government agency. If a URL ends in .uk, it is from the United Kingdom. Being aware of this as you scan your results can be very helpful. A search for domain names or country domains results in lists you can check URLs against.

- **Note the result's ranking in the list of possible Web pages**
  Search engines use **algorithms**, or mathematical formulas, to rank each Web site according to the terms used in your search query. Every search engine has a slightly different algorithm for figuring out which is the "best" Web site, but all place their best picks at the top of the list. Generally speaking, you should be able to find useful results in the first few pages of search results. If you don't, try refining your search.

- **Determine if the search engine uses directory links**
  More and more search engines are creating directories (or subject guides) of recommended Web sites on many subjects organized into categories. If a Web page is included in a directory, it usually means that it contains information that is highly relevant to the topic. Therefore, if a search engine site has included a page from a directory in the results, you can assume that it is a relevant result. Clicking a directory link sends you directly to that category of Web pages.

- **Determine if the search engine uses cached pages**
  Sometimes links to Web pages break. Search engines might not become aware of the problem until their spiders search that part of the Web again. As a result, sometimes when you click a link you get an error message. Google has many **cached pages**, which are hidden copies of indexed Web pages stored on a search engine's computer. If you click the Cached link in the description of a search result, you see the copy of the Web page with your keyword(s) highlighted, as shown in Figure A-15. Cached pages can help you find the newer or renamed or relocated version of the page, or find authors' names or other specific terms. Try a new search query using those terms to look for a new location for the updated Web page.

- **Navigate between search results pages**
  Search results are usually displayed about 10 to a page. Some searches return hundreds of pages. At Google, you navigate to a different page of results using the links located at the bottom of each results page, as shown in Figure A-16. Google, as well as some other engines, also offers search-refining options at the bottom of the page of results. Remember that the better your search strategy, the fewer pages of results you will need to examine to find relevant pages.

FIGURE A-14: Top of Google search results page

Your search query

Number of results

If you don't see these search tools, click the Show search tools link

Higher ranking results have keywords appearing in the title, on the page, and in the URL

Cached page available

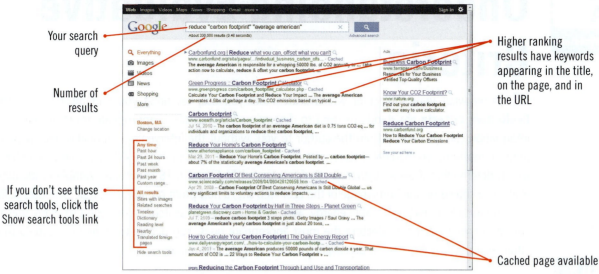

FIGURE A-15: Google's cache of a page from Carbonfund.org

Google's notification that this is a cached page

Google's image of the Web page taken previously and cached

Date this image of the page was made

URL and link to actual page

Your search query and how your keywords or phrases are highlighted on the cached page

Keywords highlighted on the page

FIGURE A-16: Bottom of a Google search results page

More pages of search results (the best results should be on the first few pages if you have created a good search strategy)

Use the Next link or the arrow to move to the next page of results

Searching the Internet Effectively

Understanding Evaluative Criteria

No matter what your subject or which search tool you use, resources you find must be evaluated. **Evaluative criteria** are standards used to determine if a Web site is appropriate for your needs. Web information can go directly from the author to you, without the intervening editorial or review process used for most printed material. This requires you to be discriminating. Figure A-17 illustrates the criteria to use in determining if a site is appropriate for your needs. Figure A-18 shows an example of identifying evaluative criteria on the home page of the EESI Web site, a non-profit organization that promotes policies that support clean and sustainable energy.  In your recent searches, you found so many sites that you are concerned about selecting the most appropriate ones. You decide to review the criteria to use when evaluating Web pages to determine which pages are appropriate.

DETAILS

Evaluative criteria include the following:

QUICK TIP

If there is an email link for the author or owner, you can write and ask questions about your research.

- **Authority and accountability**

  Knowing the author's or owner's identity is key to determining how reliable the site is. This is usually the most important criterion to apply. Consider these questions:

  - Is the author or owner clearly identified? Are qualifications and associations identified?
  - Is there contact information for the author or owner? Is there an About Us link?
  - Is there an association with a university, a government agency, or an organization? If so, are there links?
  - Has the author written in the field? Does the owner specialize in the field? What kind of results do you get from a search on the author or owner?
  - Is there a bibliography? Are resources well documented?

QUICK TIP

Nothing is wrong with selling a product or advocating an idea, but that should be stated as the site's purpose.

- **Objectivity and accuracy**

  A site's objectivity and accuracy greatly affect its appropriateness. Consider these questions:

  - Does the author state the purpose of the site? Is the content presented as fact or as opinion? Does the author show any bias?
  - Is the publisher, sponsor, or host for the site identified?

- **Organization and design**

  Great content on a page can be defeated by poor design and functionality. Attractiveness and graphic features can mask a lack of meaningful content. Consider these questions:

  - Is the site well designed and functional? Is there a site map and Help page?
  - Is it easy to navigate? Do navigational buttons and internal links work?
  - Is it searchable? Are there a variety of ways to access material?

- **Scope**

  The scope of a site is the range of topics it covers. Consider these questions:

  - Is there introductory or summary information describing the scope of the site?
  - Who is the intended audience? Is the information presented appropriately for that audience?

QUICK TIP

Check the site's home page or About page to look for dates, or try the site map to find the most logical page to check.

- **Currency**

  Currency or timeliness might or might not be an issue for your search. Consider these questions:

  - Is there a creation or revision date?
  - Are there many broken links? (This might indicate the site is not being maintained.)

FIGURE A-17: Evaluative criteria contributing to a site's appropriateness

FIGURE A-18: Identifying evaluative criteria on the EESI home page

Page name describes site and indicates **scope**

Scope indicated in page summary

Easy navigation to pages, links, and resources indicate **organization**

Link to About information indicates **authority**

Link to current information indicate **currency**

Informative graphics indicate good **design**

Link to About information indicates **authority**

Contacts information indicates **accountability** and **authority**

Understanding Wikipedia

Wikipedia.org is the largest, most popular, collaboratively built, free online encyclopedia. Since anyone can edit the information in Wikipedia, a common misconception is that Wikipedia is unreliable. In reality, comparative studies have shown that Wikipedia is actually as reliable as traditional encyclopedias. This is because when someone does accidently (or purposely) post erroneous information in Wikipedia, experts in the field typically identify and rectify the problem quickly. Although academics have been slow to accept Wikipedia as a valid source for citations, the number of scientific journals citing Wikipedia has grown significantly in recent years. As with any source, it is important to cross-check Wikipedia's information with other authoritative sources. Most Wikipedia topics provide a list of references you can use as a starting point.

Evaluating a Web Page

Every time search for information on the Internet, you must choose which Web sites to include in your research. Using the evaluative criteria in the previous lesson enables you to quickly eliminate the least useful sites so that you can focus your time and energy on the most relevant ones.  Bob the librarian mentions the Web site People & the Planet as one you might want to visit. It contains information about the effect of the growing human population on the planet. You decide to visit the site and review it using the evaluative criteria in the previous lesson.

STEPS

1. **Type peopleandplanet.net in your browser's Address bar, then press [Enter]**
   Figure A-19 illustrates the People & the Planet home page. You want to evaluate this site.

2. **Scan the page looking for indications of authority and objectivity**
   At the bottom of the page, the Contact us link leads to a page that provides a physical address, a telephone number, and an email address. The Our Supporters and See also sections list sponsors and supporters of the People & the Planet Web site. The About us link leads to a page that describes the scope of the site, and lists names of the site sponsors, partners, the editors, and the members of the editorial board and their affiliations. You decide the authority, accountability, and objectivity of this site seem excellent.

> **QUICK TIP**
> There are millions of Web pages on the Internet; it is important that you learn how to evaluate the quality of a Web page that you are unfamiliar with.

3. **Scan the page looking for indications of scope**
   There is a summary of the site's purpose on the home page. The scope is indicated from the home page links to internal resources by subject areas. The scope is also addressed on the About us page.

4. **Scan the page looking for indications of organization and currency**
   The design is attractive and functional. The links to subject areas and latest online postings show recent dates. The site map is organized and easy to use. All of the links work, there are several ways to find information, and the site is searchable. You decide this site is very well organized and current.

5. **Close all open browser tabs and windows**

Considering what others say about Web pages

Another way to evaluate a Web page is to consider how others value it. One way to determine this is to find out how many Web pages link to the page you are evaluating. If a large number of quality sites link to a page, odds are that it contains authoritative and reputable information. To reveal the sites that link to a Web page, you can use the Google link: advanced search operator; in the Google search form, type **link:** followed by the URL you want to check (for example, link:www.peopleandplanet.net). In the results page, Google will display a list of sites that link to the page you specified. You can examine the results to determine the number and quality of sites linking to the page. Another way to determine what others think about a Web page is to visit Alexa.com. Type the URL of the page you want to check in the Search text box, and then click Search. At the top of the page that appears, click Get Details to the right of the URL you typed. On the page that appears displaying statistics about the Web site, the number below the Reputation label tells you how many pages link to the site. Click that number to display a list of those pages. You can examine the list to determine the number and quality of sites linking to the page.

FIGURE A-19: People & the Planet home page

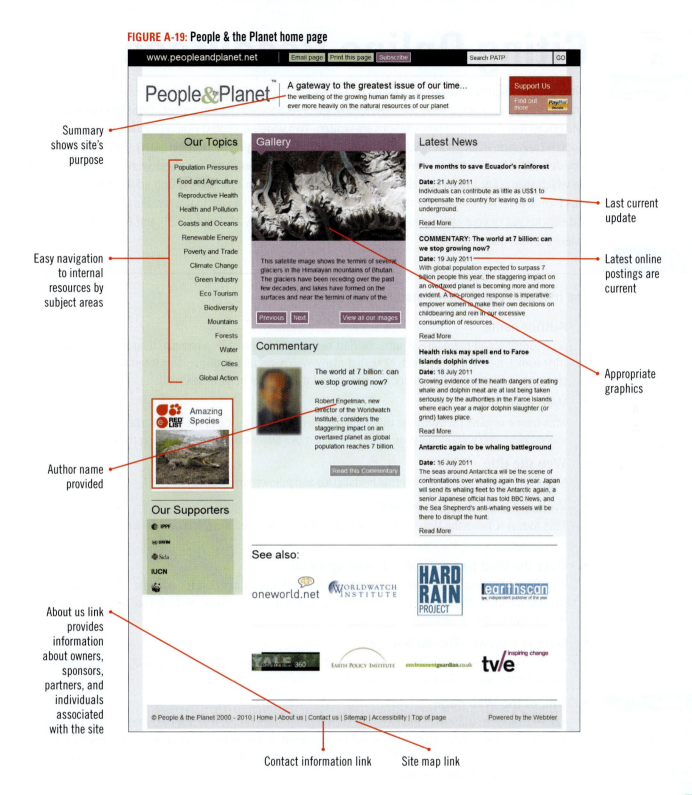

Summary shows site's purpose

Easy navigation to internal resources by subject areas

Author name provided

About us link provides information about owners, sponsors, partners, and individuals associated with the site

Last current update

Latest online postings are current

Appropriate graphics

Contact information link   Site map link

Citing Online Resources

When you use information from Web pages for classwork, you need to list them in your works cited. To present the relevant data about each site consistently, use a recognized citation format. **Citation formats** are style guides that standardize how citations are written. Two widely accepted citation formats are those of the Modern Language Association (MLA) and the American Psychological Association (APA). These style guides provide formats for all kinds of Internet information. For academic work, always check with your instructor to see which style guide format is preferred. See Table A-3 for citation tips.  Bob advises you to use the MLA format to record citations for the Web pages you are finding in a way that will make your list consistent and easy for you or your colleagues to find again. Refer to Figure A-20, Figure A-21, and Figure A-22 as you review the MLA guidelines.

DETAILS

The following are elements used in MLA citations:

- **Author name**

  MLA format for author names is surname (last name) first, followed by a comma, then the personal name (first name), followed by a period. Note that many Web pages do not display this information as clearly as the example. You might have to look to find it, and it might not be provided at all.

- **Web page title**

  MLA format requires the Web page title, which is referred to as the title of the work, to be set in italics if it is independent, and within quotation marks if it is part of a larger work, with a period at the end of the title.

- **Web site title**

  MLA format requires the Web site title be italicized and followed by a period.

- **Web site publisher or sponsor**

  MLA format requires the Web site publisher or sponsor to be listed next, followed by a comma. If no publisher or sponsor is listed, use *N.p.*

- **Date the Web page was created or updated**

  MLA format for dates is *DD Month (Abbreviation) YYYY* followed by a period, for example, 15 Oct. 2013. Note that the months with only three or four letters in their names (May, June, and July) are not abbreviated. If there is no creation or update date, use *n.d.*

- **Date you viewed the Web page**

  It is important to record the date you view a Web page because pages change frequently. Use the same format as for the date the Web page was created.

QUICK TIP

The URL for any Web page is visible in the browser's Address bar, but is not shown in Figure A-22.

- **URL of the Web page**

  The URL (Internet address) of the Web page should be included only if it would be challenging for someone to find using a search engine or if an instructor requires it. If it is included, it needs to be enclosed in angle brackets < >. If you need to break the URL into more than one line, break the line after a slash. Include a period after the right angle bracket.

Copyright and plagiarism

With the exception of works in the public domain, everything on the Internet is copyrighted, whether it is a Web page, an image, or an audio file. If you want to profit from someone else's work, you must get permission from the author or creator. Copyright law is very complex, so consult a lawyer who specializes in copyright law. If you want to use part of someone else's work in a school assignment or paper, you generally can do so under the Fair Use exemption to copyright law. "Fair use" allows students and researchers to copy or use parts of other people's work for educational purposes. Always give credit by citing the source of the material you are using. If you don't credit an author or source, you are guilty of plagiarism.

FIGURE A-20: MLA citation style format for a Web page

Element and Format	Example
Author Last Name, Author First Name.	Boswell, Wendy.
Web page title. or "Web page title."	*DIY Alternative Energy Projects.*
Web site title	*Lifehacker.*
Web site publisher or sponsor,	join.me,
Date page created or revised.	30 June 2006.
Date you viewed the Web page.	25 July 2011.
<Full URL if required>.	<http://lifehacker.com/184452/diy-alternative-energy-projects>.

FIGURE A-21: Citation in the MLA style for the Web page below in Figure A-22

Boswell, Wendy. *DIY Alternative Energy Projects. Lifehacker.* join.me, 30 June 2006. 25 July 2011. <http://lifehacker.com/184452/ diy-alternative-energy-projects>.

FIGURE A-22: Lifehacker page cited above in Figure A-21

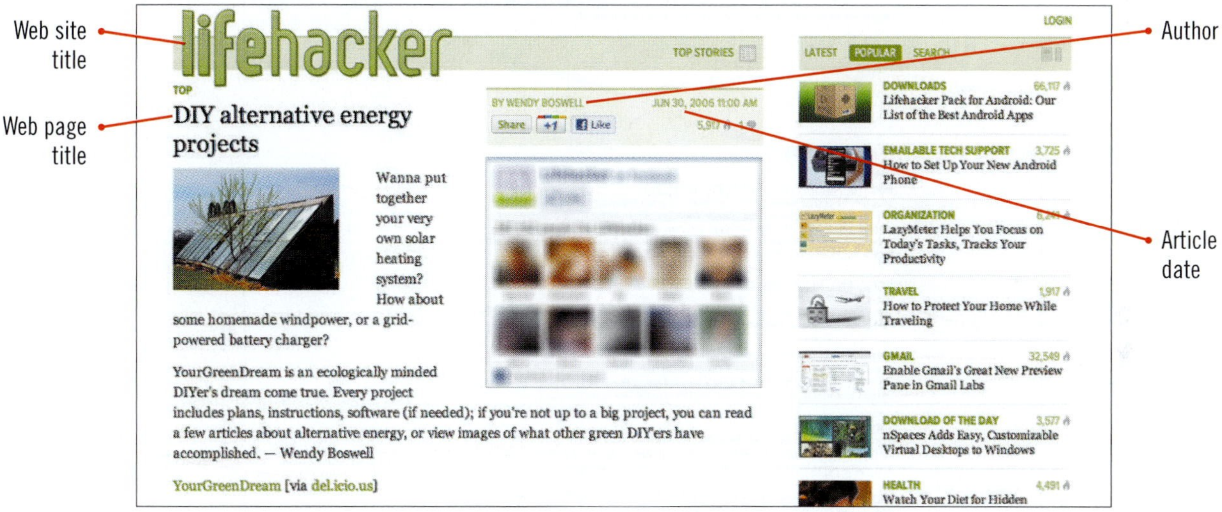

Web site title

Web page title

Author

Article date

TABLE A-3: Citation tips

citation section	tips
Author	• When authors aren't named, skip this section • If a corporate author is named, such as an association, institution, or government agency, use it in the author section
Page title	• Sometimes the title is not clear; it might be under a banner or logo at the top of the page • If you are citing the whole Web site, you can skip this section, which is for a specific page
URL	• The URL should not be underlined • Some word processors automatically underline URLs, so you might need to remove the underline
Date created/revised	• Sometimes a date can be difficult to find; it might be at the very bottom of the page • When dates aren't provided, skip this section
Date viewed	• If you print the page, the date is at the lower-right corner of your printout • If you are not printing, note the date for your citation

Practice

SAM

For current SAM information, including versions and content details, visit SAM Central (http://www.cengage.com/samcentral). If you have a SAM user profile, you may have access to hands-on instruction, practice, and assessment of the skills covered in this unit. Since various versions of SAM are supported throughout the life of this text, check with your instructor for the correct instructions and URL/Web site for accessing assignments.

Concepts Review

Label each element of Figure A-23.

FIGURE A-23

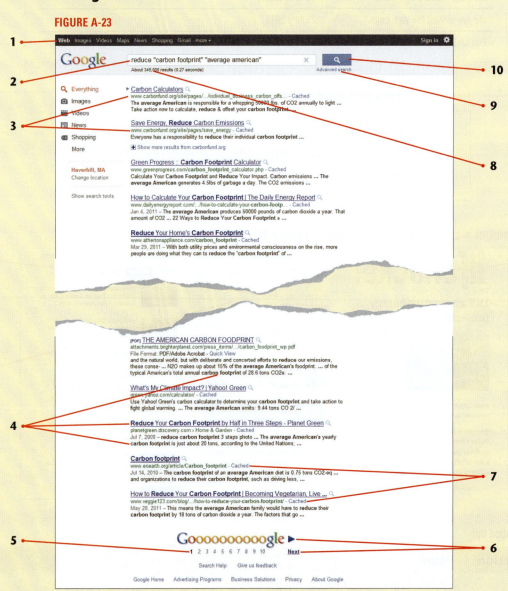

Match each term with the statement that best describes it.

11. **Deep Web**	**a.**	The order in which a search tool returns results, usually based on relevancy
12. **Cached page**	**b.**	Program that scans the Web to index the keywords in Web pages
13. **Search engine**	**c.**	Words that describe your search topic
14. **Spider**	**d.**	A Web site that locates information on the Internet by searching Web pages
15. **Keywords**	**e.**	Web pages stored in proprietary databases, specialty directories, or reference sites
16. **Result's ranking**	**f.**	Web pages that have paid for higher placement on search result pages
17. **Sponsored results**	**g.**	A copy of a Web page stored by a search engine

Select the best answer from the list of choices.

18. Which of the following do you need to apply in order to ascertain the value of information you find?

    a. Specialty search tools

    b. Search forms

    c. Evaluative criteria

    d. Stop words

19. Phrase searching helps you find:

    a. wildcards.

    b. words in the order you specify.

    c. synonyms.

    d. keywords.

20. In an MLA citation for a Web page, if you include the URL, what symbols should enclose it?

    a. { }

    b. [ ]

    c. ( )

    d. < >

21. Which term describes current popular searches?

    a. Trending searches

    b. Phrase searches

    c. Keyword searches

    d. Algorithmic searches

Skills Review

If requested by your instructor, create a document listing the answers to the questions asked in the following exercises.

1. Understand Internet search tools.

    a. Define *search query*.

    b. Describe search engines and how they work.

    c. Explain how a metasearch engine works.

    d. Describe how you find information on the deep Web.

    e. Explain how using a social media search engine is different from using a metasearch engine.

2. Create an Internet research strategy.

    a. Describe the seven steps of an effective Internet research strategy, in order.

    b. Explain the importance of translating your topic into a search query and the value of refining your query to retrieve better results.

3. Identify the right keywords.

    a. Identify the two keywords in the following search topic: *I want to find information about volunteering abroad.*

    b. Think of at least three synonyms or related words for the keywords (they might all be for the same keyword).

    c. Explain what stop words are.

Skills Review (continued)

4. Perform a basic search.

    a. Go to the Google search form at **google.com**.

    b. Conduct a search for *volunteer abroad*. Note the total number of results returned.

5. Add keywords.

    a. Examine only the first page of results from the search you conducted using the search query *volunteer abroad* (in Skills Review 4b). How many useful results are listed?

    b. Modify the search query by adding the keyword *summer*, and then conduct the new search. Examine only the first page of results again. How many useful results appear now?

    c. Modify the search query by adding the keyword *student*, and then conduct the new search. Once again, examine only the first page of results. Now how many useful results appear?

    d. Modify the search once more by adding the keyword *college*. How many useful results appear on the first page of results?

6. Use phrase searching.

    a. Replace the search query in the Google search engine with *"volunteer abroad"*, and then conduct the new search.

    b. Examine the first page of search results. Is the number of results different from the search you conducted using the same search query without the quotation marks (in Skills Review 4b)?

7. Analyze search results.

    a. Replace the search query in the Google search engine with *volunteer*, and then conduct the search.

    b. Examine the first page of results. How many results were returned?

    c. How many results contain your keyword in the URL?

    d. How many results listed on the first page of results paid to be listed there? Is each sponsored result from a different company or organization? Do any of the sponsored results also appear in the list of results that are not sponsored?

    e. How many of the results on the first page of results are available as cached results from Google?

8. Understand evaluative criteria.

    a. Define *evaluative criteria*.

    b. According to the text, what are the five things to consider when evaluating a Web page?

    c. What is one way you can determine the credibility of an author of a Web page?

9. Evaluate a Web page.

    a. Go to **idealist.org**.

    b. Evaluate this Web page for authority and accountability. What areas of the page did you use to do this?

    c. Is this Web page objective and accurate? Does it show any bias? How did you determine this?

    d. Describe the organization of the Web site. Is it well organized in your opinion?

    e. Describe the scope of this Web site. How did you determine this?

    f. Is the Web page current? How do you know?

10. Cite online resources.

    a. Select one of the Web pages returned by one of your searches.

    b. How would you write the citation for this Web page using MLA format?

Independent Challenge 1

If requested by your instructor, create a document listing the answers to the questions asked in the following exercises.

Your friend is considering a career change and wants you to help with a Web search. He wants to find information about jobs in computing in the greater New York City area.

    a. Identify the topic statement for this Web search.

    b. Identify the keywords in the topic statement.

    c. Identify at least three related words for the keywords.

    d. From all of your keywords, compose a search query. Include at least one search phrase in the query.

    e. Go to **bing.com**.

    f. Perform your search, and note the number of search results returned.

Independent Challenge 2

If requested by your instructor, create a document listing the answers to the questions asked in the following exercises.

You want to search the Internet for information on a topic of your choosing.

    a. Decide on a topic, and identify the topic statement.

    b. Note your keywords and any synonyms or related terms.

    c. Create a basic search query, choose a search engine, and perform a search.

    d. Analyze the search results using the skills you learned in this unit, and then refine your search query so that it returns fewer results.

    e. Create an MLA citation for one of your resulting pages.

Advanced Challenge Exercise

- Go to **google.com** and conduct a search for information about World War II. Did you use *World War II* as the search query or did you use *WWII*? Repeat the search using the other search query. Did the number of results differ significantly? Note the first result on the first page.
- Refine your search so you are searching for information about the paratroopers in World War II. Did you use a search phrase? Repeat the search using a search phrase if you did not already do so, or without using a search phrase if you already used one. How many fewer results were returned when you used the search phrase? Is the first result on the first page different from the previous search?
- Refine your search to include information about the Battle of Normandy. Did the number of results decrease significantly? Did the first result on the first page change?
- In the left pane of the Google results page, click the Timeline link. Describe how the results changed.

Independent Challenge 3

If requested by your instructor, create a document listing the answers to the questions asked in the following exercises.

You want to find information about the music of South Africa. You decide to use phrase searching to narrow your search results.

    a. Go to **google.com**, and then conduct a search for *South Africa music*. Note the number of results.

    b. Conduct a search for *zulu music*.

    c. Conduct a search for *crossover music*. Note the number of results.

    d. Conduct a phrase search for *"South Africa" zulu "crossover music"*. Note the number of results.

    e. Which search yielded the fewest results? Why?

    f. In a new browser window or tab, conduct the same search for *"South Africa" zulu "crossover music"* on **bing.com**. Compare the number of results to the number found when you conducted this search on Google. Why do the number of results differ?

Advanced Challenge Exercise

- In the tab or window containing the Google results, click the Advanced search link below the Search button, and then use the option to restrict the search to Web sites in the region of South Africa. Note the number of results.

- In the tab or window containing the Google results, use the Advanced Search page to add a restriction to the domain .za. Note the number of results. Also, examine the revised search phrase in the Search text box, and note the search operator and keyword that was added.

- In the tab or window containing the Bing results, click the Advanced link above the results list, and then use the option to restrict the search to Web sites in South Africa. Note the number of results. Also, examine the revised search phrase in the Search text box, and note the search operator and keyword that was added.

- In the tab or window containing the Bing results, use the Advanced Search page to add a restriction to the domain .za. Note the number of results. Also, examine the revised search phrase in the Search text box, and note the search operator and keyword that was added.

- In the tab or window containing the Bing results, delete the search operator and keyword from the Search text box that restricted the search to the region of South Africa. Note the number of results.

Real Life Independent Challenge

If requested by your instructor, create a document listing the answers to the questions asked in the following exercises.

In today's job market, many people find that technical skills, while necessary, are not sufficient for career advancement. Employability skills are equally important to maintaining a job and improving one's position. You decide to research how to improve your employability skills.

a. Go to **google.com**.

b. Conduct a search using the keyword *employability*. Examine the results on the first few pages.

c. Refine your search query to *employability skills*, and then search again. Examine the search results. Do you see many results that might give you information on improving your employability skills?

d. Modify your search query again to *improving employability skills*, and then repeat the search. Are the results more targeted to improving employability skills?

e. Modify your search query so it is a search phrase: *"improving employability skills"*. Conduct the search and examine the results. Do any of the results mention *soft skills*, *interpersonal skills*, or *emotional IQ*?

f. Choose one of the phrases mentioned in exercise e, add it to your search query, and then conduct the search. Did this yield more relevant results?

g. Delete your search query, and then conduct a new search using two of the phrases mentioned in exercise e. Does this search give you the same list of results, or are they different?

h. Finally, after reviewing the results you received in the searches you conducted in this Independent Challenge, create a new search query that contains search phrases and keywords that produce results that will help you advance in your field. For example, if you are in marketing, you could add *"marketing manager"* to your search query. Conduct the search and examine the results.

Visual Workshop

A friend gives you a printout of the Web page shown in Figure A-24, but the URL that should be at the bottom of the page is torn off. You decide to find the page from the information on the printout. Using Google, search for the page. Create a citation for the page in the MLA format. (Note that the image displayed on the page might differ from the one shown here.) If requested by your instructor, print or save this page of results.

FIGURE A-24

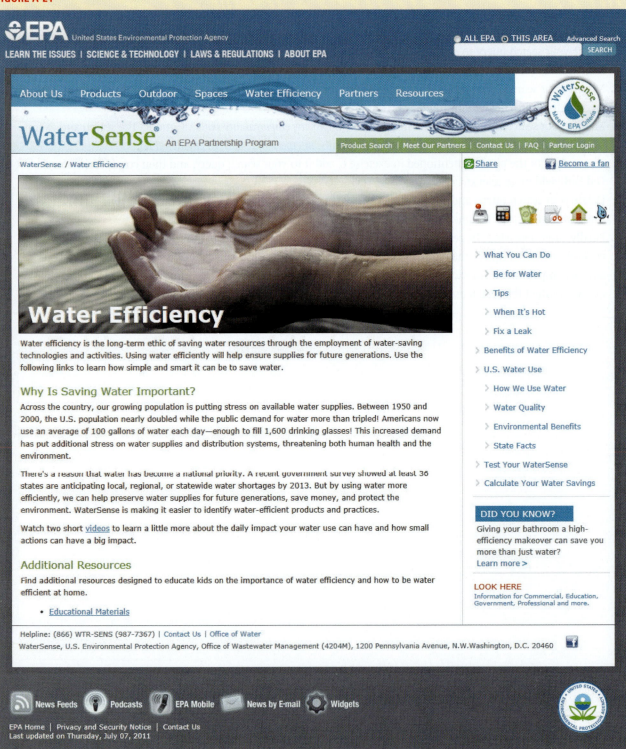

Constructing Complex Searches

**Files You
Will Need:**
No files needed.

Many search engines allow **complex search queries**, or advanced searches, which use special connecting words and symbols called Boolean operators. Search filters provide another method to narrow your search by limiting its scope to a specific part of the Web. Combining complex queries with search filters lets you focus more exactly on the information you need. You can also use metasearch engines to simultaneously search the indexes of multiple search engines. The city planning team requests information on alternative energy-related associations in the region and on alternative energy use in surrounding states and provinces. As you design search strategies, Bob, your friend the reference librarian, provides information on Boolean operators and filters you can use to help refine your searches.

OBJECTIVES

Understand Boolean operators

Narrow a search with the AND operator

Expand a search with the OR operator

Restrict a search with the NOT operator

Use multiple Boolean operators

Search with filters

Combine Boolean operators and filters

Use advanced search operators

Use metasearch engines

Understanding Boolean Operators

The English language uses **syntax**, a special set of rules, for combining words to form grammatical sentences. Search engines use **Boolean logic**, a special mathematical syntax, to perform complex searches. In Boolean logic, keywords act like nouns in a sentence. Like nouns, keywords represent subjects. You use **Boolean operators**, connecting words such as AND, OR, and NOT, to tell a search engine how to interpret your complex searches. Boolean operators work like conjunctions in a sentence, defining connections between keywords. Boolean logic is usually illustrated with Venn diagrams. 🎨 Bob explains that you can create more efficient complex searches when you understand how Boolean operators connect keywords. He provides information on Boolean operators and on Venn diagrams, which illustrate how the operators work.

DETAILS

To review Boolean operators and Venn diagrams:

QUICK TIP
If you have trouble deciding which Boolean operator to use in your search strategy, sketch a Venn diagram labeled with your terms and it will become clear.

- **Venn diagrams**

  Venn diagrams are drawings that visually represent searches using Boolean operators. For example, consider the Venn diagrams in Figure B-1. The rectangle represents the World Wide Web. Circles inside the rectangle represent groups of related Web pages, called **sets**. One circle represents a search for pages containing the word *cats*. Another circle represents a search for *dogs*. If the circles overlap, the overlapping area represents pages that are retrieved by both searches. This overlapping area is called the **intersection** of the sets. If you limit your search to pages containing *both* of the words, the search results are represented by the intersection of these two circles. If you expand your search to pages containing *either* word, the search results are represented by both full circles. This is called the **union** of the two sets. If you restrict your search to pages containing one word, but *not* the other one, this search is represented by the part of one circle that does *not* overlap the other one. This search excludes one set from the other. Table B-1 shows how the searches illustrated by the Venn diagrams are entered and interpreted.

QUICK TIP
Always use CAPITAL LETTERS when typing any Boolean operator. If you type the word *and* in lowercase, it will either be interpreted as a keyword or ignored as a stop word.

- **Boolean operators**

  Boolean operators, AND, OR, and NOT, expand, narrow, or restrict searches based on Boolean logic. Boolean logic, or Boolean algebra, is the field of mathematics that defines how Boolean operators manipulate large sets of data. Search engines handle large data sets and use Boolean logic to perform complex searches, usually called advanced searches. Boolean operators act as commands to the search engine. How they connect keywords and phrases tells the search engine how to interpret your search and thus helps you retrieve the results you want. Boolean operators control which keywords *must* be on the Web page (**AND**), which *may or may not* be on the Web page (**OR**), and which keyword *must not* be on the Web page (**NOT**).

QUICK TIP
If you're unsure about using Boolean operators at a new search engine or unsure about its default operator, refer to the engine's Help pages.

- **Default Boolean operator**

  Search engines insert Boolean operators into multiple word searches whether you supply them in the search query or not. The operator that the engine automatically uses is called the **default operator**. Most search engines default to AND. Others default to OR. When you search two or more words, some engines assume you want the words in a phrase and treat the query as if you used quotation marks. Being aware of an engine's default operator is important to create the best search strategy for that engine.

- **Where to use Boolean operators**

  Some search engines allow Boolean searching on the basic search page, but some allow it only on the advanced search page. In the past, almost all search engines recognized all Boolean operators when typed in all capital letters in the Search text box on the basic search page. Now many only recognize them if you use the advanced search page's specialized text boxes. Some do not allow the use of the English words AND or NOT, but do allow the plus sign (+) or minus sign (–) instead.

FIGURE B-1: Venn diagrams comparing search results for six searches

All pages on the Web

Set of pages on the Web containing the word *cats*

Set of pages on the Web containing the word *dogs*

cats

dogs

cats

Intersection of the two sets (fewer results because the search was limited by AND)

cats

dogs

cats **AND** dogs

cats

dogs

cats **OR** dogs

Union of the two sets (more results because the search was expanded by OR)

Exclusion of the dogs set (fewer results because the search was limited by NOT)

cats

dogs

cats **NOT** dogs

cats

dogs

dogs **NOT** cats

Exclusion of the cats set (fewer results because the search was limited by NOT)

TABLE B-1: How the searches represented in Figure B-1 might be entered in and interpreted by a search engine

search	operator	search interpreted as asking for
cats	*<no operator>*	Web pages containing the word *cats*
dogs	*<no operator>*	Web pages containing the word *dogs*
cats dogs	AND	Web pages containing *both* words (AND is the assumed operator in most search tools, so you rarely type it)
cats OR dogs	OR	Web pages containing *either* word
cats NOT dogs	NOT	Web pages containing the word *cats* but *not* the word *dogs*
dogs -cats	NOT	Web pages containing the word *dogs* but *not* the word *cats*

Remembering Boolean logic

You might remember Boolean logic and Venn diagrams from a math class. An Englishman named George Boole (1815–1864) invented a form of symbolic logic called Boolean algebra, which is used in the fields of mathematics, logic, computer science, and artificial intelligence. John

Venn (1843–1923), also an Englishman, used his diagrams to explain visually what Boole had described symbolically—the intersection, union, and exclusion of sets. Little did they know then that they were creating the foundation of the language that Internet search engines use today.

Internet Research

Narrowing a Search with the AND Operator

The Boolean operator AND (sometimes indicated with a plus sign) is a powerful operator that limits or narrows your results. When you connect keywords in your search with AND, you are telling the search engine that *both* of the keywords must be on every Web page, not just one or the other. Each AND added to your search query further narrows the search results to fewer pages, and these results pages will be more relevant than those returned by a broader, or less specific, search. A good time to use AND is when your initial keyword or phrase search finds too many irrelevant results. You can also use AND to force the search engine to include a stop word in the search query. Remember that most search engines use AND as their default operator, which means that the engine assumes you mean to connect keywords with AND unless you tell it otherwise. Google actually treats AND as a stop word, despite the capitalization. However, you still might encounter some search tools in which you have to use the plus sign or AND. If you're unsure, check the search tool's Help page. Table B-2 lists several examples of search queries using the AND operator. Bob explains that to search for solar energy associations near Portland, you can use the AND operator to narrow your search, even though you will not type AND between your keywords.

STEPS

1. **Start your Web browser, type google.com in your browser's Address bar, then press [Enter]**

   The Google search form opens. To illustrate how Boolean operators can broaden or narrow a search, first you will search for Web pages that contain the phrase *solar energy association*.

2. **Type "solar energy association" in the Search text box, then click the Search button** 🔍

   Note the number of results. Now you will search for pages that contain the text *Portland*.

   QUICK TIP
   You can but do not have to capitalize proper names in search text boxes.

3. **Delete the search query in the Search text box, type portland, then click** 🔍

   Note the number of results. To find the pages that contain both the phrase *"solar energy association"* and the text *Portland*, you would have to read as many Web pages as these two sets of results combined. Instead, you can create a search query using a Boolean operator to identify these pages for you.

4. **Delete the search query in the Search text box, type "solar energy association" portland, then click** 🔍

   This search, using the assumed AND operator, narrows your results to *solar energy association* pages that also contain *Portland*. Figure B-2 shows a Venn diagram of this search, and Figure B-3 shows the search results page.

Using the plus sign

The plus sign is useful to prevent a search engine from ignoring a stop word. It also functions like quotation marks around a phrase. Whether using quotation marks around a phrase or the plus sign before a single keyword, you are forcing the search engine to look for a word it would normally ignore. For example, *Henry +I* produces the same results as *"Henry I"*. When you use the plus sign, you must leave a space in front of it, but no space between it and the keyword it is connecting to; for example, *+the goal orr* (used to force inclusion of a stop word)

and music *+blues +memphis* (used as the Boolean AND). Note that using the plus sign in Google also restricts searches to results that contain the exact keyword you typed. This is because Google automatically applies synonyms or other close matches to keywords. For example, Google will return pages with the keyword *childcare* when you enter *child care* or *California history* for the query *ca history*. However, if you type the plus symbol in front of a keyword, Google searches only for pages that precisely match the keyword.

FIGURE B-2: Venn diagram illustrating results for *"solar energy association"* AND *portland*

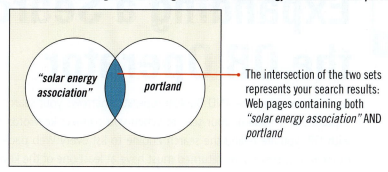

The intersection of the two sets represents your search results: Web pages containing both *"solar energy association"* AND *portland*

FIGURE B-3: Google search results for *"solar energy association"* AND *portland*

Your search query

Number of results

Highlighted keywords in the results

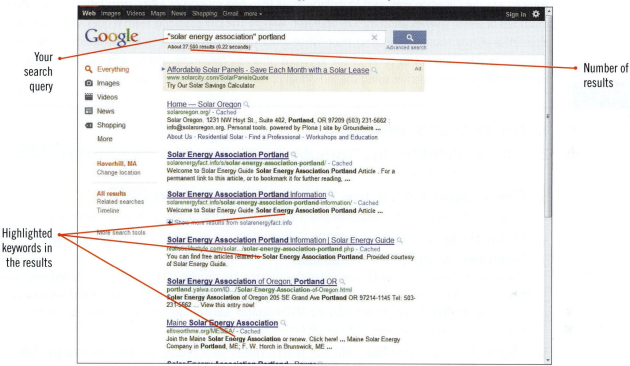

TABLE B-2: Sample search queries using the Boolean operator AND

example	result
solar panels	Assumed AND between keywords returns pages that contain the word *solar* and the word *panels*
"solar panels" "wind turbines"	Assumed AND between search phrases returns pages that contain the phrase *solar panels* and the phrase *wind turbines*
+and i love her	Forces inclusion of the stop word "and"

Keeping a search diary

It is a good idea to log searches as you perform them, noting the Boolean operators used in your search statements, and the number of results returned. This helps you remember what searches you have tried and which ones yielded useful results. Your search logs can also be used by others to reproduce your search results.

Constructing Complex Searches

Expanding a Search with the OR Operator

As you have seen, the AND Boolean operator narrows your search. Conversely, the Boolean operator OR expands, or broadens, your search. When you connect keywords or search phrases in your search query with OR, you are telling the search engine to list every Web page that contains any of the keywords. In other words, every page returned must have at least one of the keywords on it but it doesn't need to have more than one. Each OR added to your search expands the search to include more Web pages. A good time to use OR is when your initial search finds too few results. Refer to the synonyms or related words you identified when developing your search strategy and connect one or more to your search query with OR. You can also use OR when you want to include more than one spelling of a keyword. Table B-3 lists several examples of search queries using the OR operator. 🎨 The city planning team requests information on alternative energy sources. Checking your list of synonyms and related words, you decide to perform a complex search using OR to connect the keyword phrases *"renewable energy"* and *"alternative energy"*. First you will perform searches using the individual phrases so you can compare results.

STEPS

1. **Clear the Google Search text box**

2. **In the Search text box, type "renewable energy", then click the Search button** ▢
   Note the number of results.

3. **Clear the Search text box, type "alternative energy", then click** ▢
   Again, note the number of results. Now you will include both search phrases in your search query.

4. **Click in the Search text box, edit the search query so it reads "renewable energy" "alternative energy", then click** ▢
   The number of results returned is fewer than the previous two searches. This search requires that every page returned contains both phrases. Although you did not type it, the search engine interpreted your search as if you had connected your phrases with the AND operator. You want to expand your search, not narrow it, so you will connect the phrases with the OR operator.

5. **Click in the Search text box, edit the search query so it reads "renewable energy" OR "alternative energy", then click** ▢
   This search requires that every page returned contains only one of your phrases, but not necessarily both. The number of results is greater than the number of results returned when you used the AND operator. Figure B-4 illustrates your search results with a Venn diagram, and Figure B-5 shows the search results page. You might reasonably expect the number of results to equal the sum of your first two searches. However, this is rarely the case because some Web pages contain both phrases and the results page eliminates many duplicates.

FIGURE B-4: Venn diagram illustrating results using the Boolean operator OR

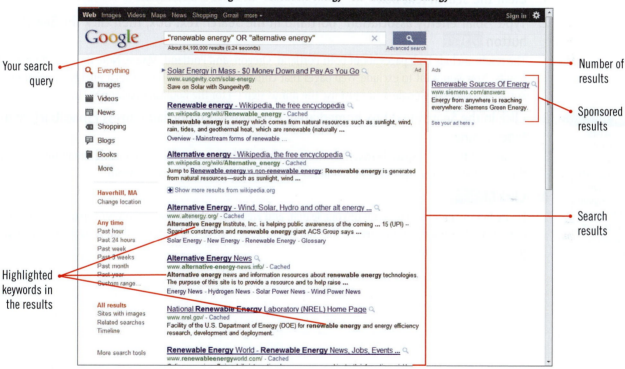

The union of the two sets represents your results: Web pages containing either *"renewable energy"* OR *"alternative energy"*

FIGURE B-5: Search results in Google for *"renewable energy"* OR *"alternative energy"*

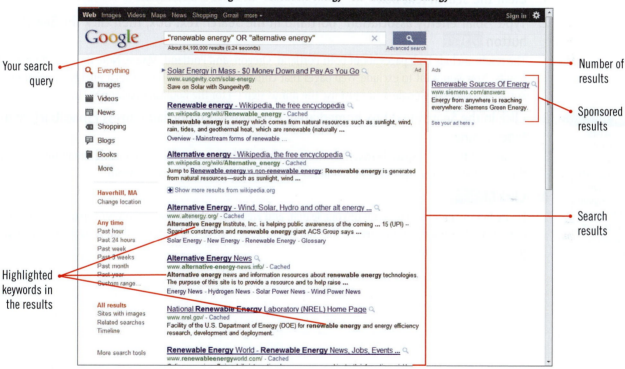

TABLE B-3: Sample search queries using the Boolean operator OR

example	result
oregon **OR** *"pacific northwest"*	Broadens search and returns more results
renewable **OR** *sustainable* **OR** *alternative*	Combines synonyms and returns more results
draft **OR** *draught*	Expands search to include both spellings and returns more results

Constructing Complex Searches

Restricting a Search with the NOT Operator

The Boolean operator NOT (sometimes indicated with a minus sign, AND NOT, or ANDNOT) excludes the keyword or search phrase that follows it. Therefore, NOT narrows or limits your search by not returning pages that contain the excluded terms. If you scan the first couple of results pages and see numerous irrelevant pages returned, locate any words or phrases that your desired search results should not contain, and then modify your search query by adding these words or phrases with NOT. Table B-4 lists several examples of search queries using NOT. 🎨 Your search results for solar energy associations in Portland included Web pages about both Portland, Oregon, and Portland, Maine. You know that one way to narrow the search would be to use the search phrase *"Portland, Oregon"*. However, you don't want to exclude pages that mention Portland, but don't mention Oregon, so instead, you will use Boolean NOT logic to construct your search query. Before trying NOT, you decide to search without it to compare results.

STEPS

1. **Clear the Search text box**

2. **Type "solar energy association" portland in the Search text box, then click the Search button** 🔍

   The results include Web pages about both Portland, Oregon, and Portland, Maine. Note the total number of results. Now you want to exclude Web pages that contain information about a solar energy association in Portland, Maine. In Google, you must use the minus sign (–) for the Boolean operator NOT.

QUICK TIP
Words you exclude from search results using NOT or a minus sign might still appear in sponsored results; this is a good reminder that sponsored results are not the same as actual search results.

3. **Click in the Search text box immediately after the word portland, press [Spacebar], then type –maine**

   Be sure not to leave a space between the minus sign and the word *Maine*. When using the minus sign (–), there must always be a space before it and no space between it and the next keyword.

4. **Click** 🔍

   Figure B-6 shows a Venn diagram of your search, and Figure B-7 shows the search results page. The number of results is less than your first search that did not include the NOT operator, and none of the results pages include the word *Maine*.

FIGURE B-6: Venn diagram illustrating results for the search *"solar energy association"* AND *portland* NOT *maine*

Every page in this set (*maine*) is excluded from your results

The part of the intersection of the sets *"solar energy association"* and *portland* that does not intersect with the third set *maine* represents your results: Web pages containing *"solar energy association"* AND *portland* NOT *maine*

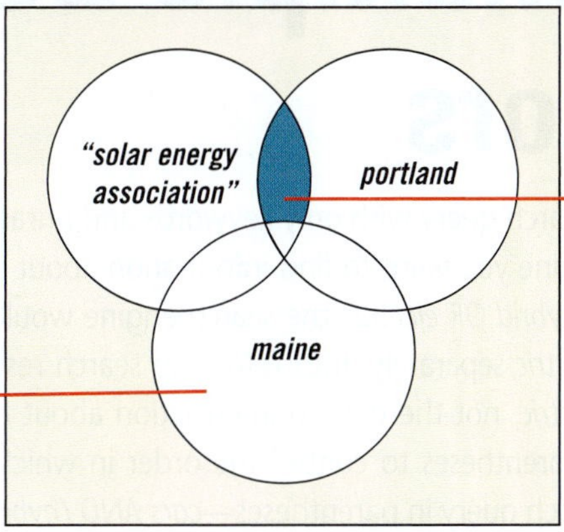

FIGURE B-7: Search results in Google for *"solar energy association"* AND *portland* NOT *maine*

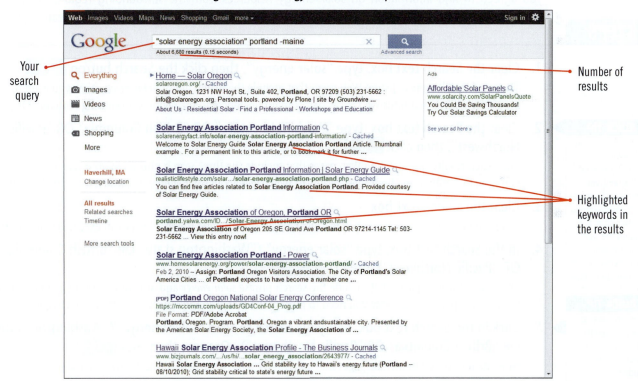

Your search query

Number of results

Highlighted keywords in the results

TABLE B-4: Sample search queries using the Boolean operator NOT

example	result
"alternative energy" –*geothermal*	Returns fewer results because the keyword *geothermal* is excluded
cardinals –*"st. louis"* –*arizona* –*catholic*	Excludes nonrelevant contexts from results

Using Multiple Boolean Operators

When you construct a search query with only keywords and phrases, search engines process it from left to right. For example, imagine you want to find information about hybrid cars or electric cars. If you simply entered the query *cars hybrid OR electric*, the search engine would first process *cars AND hybrid* and then process the keyword *electric* separately, thus returning search results about *hybrid cars* or the pages containing the keyword *electric*, not the desired information about hybrid cars or electric cars. To solve this problem, you can use parentheses to control the order in which a query is processed. In our example, enclosing part of the search query in parentheses—*cars AND (hybrid OR electric)*—causes the search engine to pair *cars AND hybrid* as well as *cars AND electric*, giving your desired search results. Using parentheses can have a significant impact on search results. Figure B-8 illustrates results in which the search tool read the query and performed the search from left to right, producing irrelevant results. Figure B-9 illustrates results in which the order of operation was forced using parentheses, producing relevant results. See Table B-5 for steps to use in planning a complex search for alternative energy in British Columbia or Alberta, Canada, excluding pages that mention geothermal energy. 🎨 In your last team meeting, you agreed to find information on solar energy resources from the surrounding region, not just in Portland, Oregon. Bob suggests you combine Boolean operators to construct a complex search query.

STEPS

1. **Clear the Search text box, type "solar energy", then click the Search button** 🔍

   The search results appear listing Web pages that include the search phrase *solar energy*. Now you want to create a search query that finds Web pages that contain references to the region surrounding Portland, Oregon.

   QUICK TIP
   If you had used only the keyword *Washington* in your search query, your results would contain many pages referring to Washington, D.C. Including the word *state* in the search phrase returns results for Washington state.

2. **Clear the Search text box, type "Washington state" OR "British Columbia" OR "Pacific Northwest", then click** 🔍

   The search results appear listing Web pages that include the three search phrases in your search query. Now you need to combine and limit these results to Web pages about solar energy that also refer to the Northwest.

3. **Clear the Search text box**

   You need to clear the Search text box because Google ignores parentheses added to an executed search query.

4. **In the Search text box, type "solar energy" ("Washington state" OR "British Columbia" OR "Pacific Northwest"), then click** 🔍

   The results list Web pages that include the search phrase *solar energy* and at least one of the search phrases between the parentheses. Now you need to modify the search so the results do not include Oregon.

   QUICK TIP
   Be sure to leave no space between the minus sign and the keyword to be excluded.

5. **Click in the Search text box, edit your search to read "solar energy" ("Washington state" OR "British Columbia" OR "Pacific Northwest") –Oregon, then click** 🔍

   Now the results do not include pages that contain *Oregon*. Figure B-10 illustrates the results.

Using multiple Boolean operators instead of advanced search forms

Most search tools contain advanced search pages, which can be convenient for performing complex searches. If you ever find yourself unsure about what to do when using these pages, return to these basic steps: identifying keywords and related words; sketching Venn diagrams to recall how the Boolean operators work; and writing down your search query using the Boolean operators AND, OR, and NOT.

Understanding Boolean logic helps you create successful online search strategies when you use the convenience of advanced search pages. However, the more complex your searches become, the more likely you will need to go back to the basic search page where you have more control over your search statement, thus reducing the chances of inadvertent logic errors.

FIGURE B-8: Venn diagram illustrating the search: *constitution AND American OR "United States"*

Order of operation was not forced with parentheses, so the search engine read the operators from left to right, resulting in the search: *constitution* AND *American* OR *"United States"*

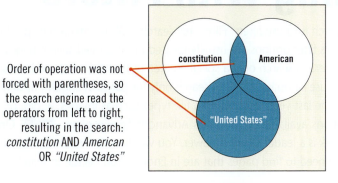

FIGURE B-9: Venn diagram illustrating the search: *constitution AND (American OR "United States")*

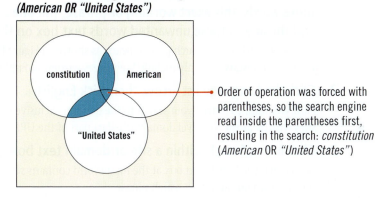

Order of operation was forced with parentheses, so the search engine read inside the parentheses first, resulting in the search: *constitution (American OR "United States")*

FIGURE B-10: Venn diagram illustrating the search *"solar energy" AND ("Washington state" OR "British Columbia" OR "Pacific Northwest") NOT Oregon*

Web pages containing (*"Washington state"* OR *"British Columbia"* OR *"Pacific Northwest"*) AND *"solar energy"* NOT *Oregon*

Web pages containing *"Washington state"* OR *"British Columbia"* OR *"Pacific Northwest"*

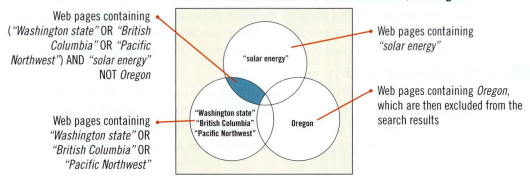

Web pages containing *"solar energy"*

Web pages containing *Oregon*, which are then excluded from the search results

TABLE B-5: Planning a complex search with multiple Boolean operators

step	example
1. Identify the first concept. Use keywords, synonyms, and related words. Connect them with OR and surround them with parentheses.	(British Columbia OR BC OR Alberta)
2. Identify the second concept. Use keywords, synonyms, and related words. Connect them with OR and surround them with parentheses.	(Canada OR Canadian)
3. Identify the third concept. Quotation marks identify this as a phrase.	"alternative energy"
4. Identify the fourth concept. You want this word excluded from your results, so you use the Boolean operator NOT.	–geothermal
5. Connect all of your concepts into one search statement.	(British Columbia OR BC OR Alberta) AND (Canada OR Canadian) AND "alternative energy" -geothermal

Constructing Complex Searches

Searching with Filters

Another way to refine a search is to use filters. Filters tell search tools to screen out specified types of Web pages or files. A search tool's filter options are usually located on advanced search pages. As you develop your search strategy, use filters to search only a specified area of the Web or to exclude specified areas of the Web. For example, you use language filters to search only for pages in English, or date filters to search only for pages updated in the last year, or for certain file types such as images, audio, or video. Table B-6 lists examples of filter options available on Google's Advanced Search page. 🎨 One of your team members read that Denmark is a leader in wind power. You want to view some Danish sites, but because you don't read Danish, you need to find pages that are in English. You decide to search using filters.

STEPS

1. **Click the Advanced search link to the right of the Search text box, then clear the all these words, this exact wording or phrase, the one or more of these words text boxes, and the any of these unwanted words text box on the Advanced Search page**

   The Google Advanced Search page appears, as shown in Figure B-11. First, you want to set up a filter so that your search results will only include Web pages written in English.

2. **Click the Language list arrow, then click English**

   Now you want to restrict your search to the domain exclusive to Denmark, that is, Web pages stored on Web sites with *dk* as the top-level domain (the last part of the URL).

3. **Click in the Search within a site or domain text box, then type .dk**

   Notice that the Search text box at the top of form contains *site:.dk*. This is how this filter appears in a search query. Now you can type a search phrase.

4. **Click in the this exact wording or phrase text box, then type wind power**

   In the Advanced Search form, you do not need to type the search phrase within quotation marks. This specialized text box interprets any words typed here as a phrase, so quotation marks are assumed. In the Search text box at the top of the form, the search phrase appears automatically within quotation marks, and the final search query appears as *"wind power" site:.dk*. Google does not add the language filter to the search query; that filter will appear on the results page as a selected option under the Search text box.

QUICK TIP
Some search engines display the language filter (lang:) as part of the search query.

5. **Click Advanced Search**

   The search is executed and the results appear on a results page. Figure B-12 illustrates the results in a Venn diagram. The Web pages returned contain the phrase *wind power*, are in English, as indicated by the selected Search English pages label that appears under the Search text box and the Search English pages link (in red) that appears in the left pane above the search option links, and are from Denmark's domain.

TABLE B-6: Examples of filters on Google's Advanced Search page

filter	what it does
Language	Limits search to pages written in a specified language (English, French, etc.)
File type	Limits search to pages in a specified format (.pdf, .xls, .doc, .ppt, etc.)
Date	Limits search to pages updated, crawled, and indexed in a specified time period (1 day, 1 week, 1 month, etc.)
Search within a site or domain	Limits search to pages only with a specified domain or within a specified site
Where your keywords show up	Limits search to pages containing your keywords in a specified location (URL, title, text, links on the page, etc.)
Usage rights	Limits search to pages covered by the Creative Commons license (still check usage rights for each page)
Region	Limits search to pages originating from a specified region or country (not all URLs identify a country)
Numeric range	Limits search to pages containing numbers in a specified range

FIGURE B-11: Boolean logic and filters on Google's Advanced Search form

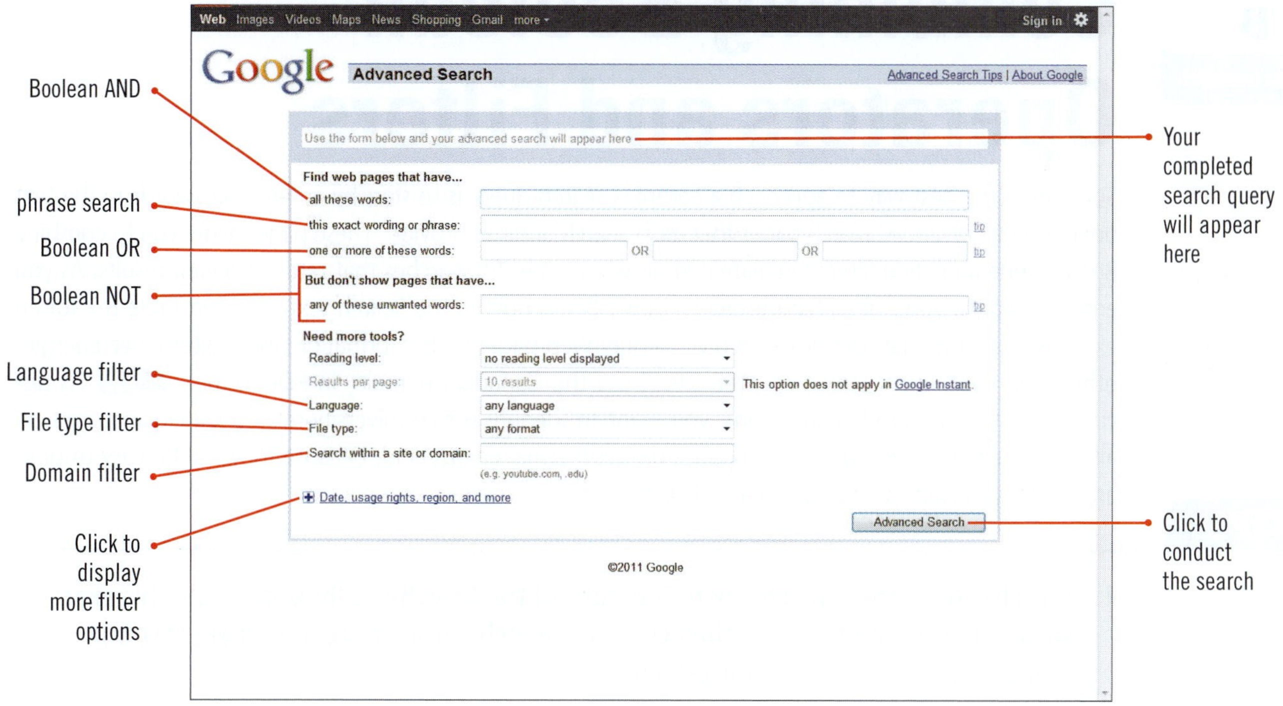

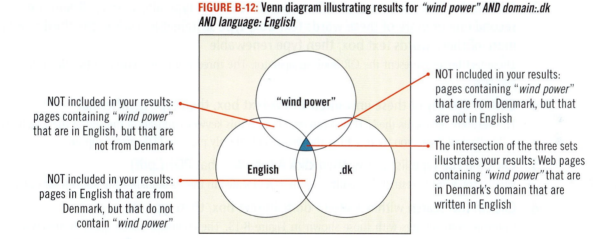

Boolean AND

phrase search

Boolean OR

Boolean NOT

Language filter

File type filter

Domain filter

Click to display more filter options

Your completed search query will appear here

Click to conduct the search

FIGURE B-12: Venn diagram illustrating results for *"wind power"* AND domain:.dk AND language: English

NOT included in your results: pages containing *"wind power"* that are in English, but that are not from Denmark

NOT included in your results: pages in English that are from Denmark, but that do not contain *"wind power"*

NOT included in your results: pages containing *"wind power"* that are from Denmark, but that are not in English

The intersection of the three sets illustrates your results: Web pages containing *"wind power"* that are in Denmark's domain that are written in English

"wind power"

English

.dk

Filtering domains in the URL

When you apply a domain filter, the search is restricted to URLs hosted in the specified domain as indicated by the letters after the period in the URL. Most Web sites in the United States have URLs that end in three letters that represent the type of organization hosting the Web site. For example, university sites end in .edu, government sites end in .gov, commercial sites end in .com, and nonprofits end in .org. Others include .biz, .pro, .info, and .net. In addition, .us, .coop, .museum, and .name are available. Many Web sites located in other countries use two-letter country codes: Canada's domain is .ca; the United Kingdom's domain is .uk; and Japan's domain is .jp. Any of these codes can limit search results when using a domain filter. For a graphical listing of the two-letter country codes, go to the ICANN (Internet Corporation for Assigned Names and Numbers) Web site at icann.org/en/maps/root-whois.htm. You can find other sites listing the two-letter country codes by searching for *countries* AND *domains*.

Combining Boolean Operators and Filters

Sometimes the best way to approach a complex search query is to start by entering keywords in the text boxes on the advanced search pages that most search engines provide. These pages allow you to combine Boolean operators and filters to create complex, very specific searches that return relevant results. As you enter keywords, you can watch the search query being built in the Search text box. See Table B-7 for an example of planning a complex search to identify Web pages with information about alternative energies other than geothermal stored on Web sites from the Canadian domain, in PDF format. As discussed with your city planning team, you want to identify some university-related Canadian pages on alternative energies. You don't need pages on geothermal energy and, because they will be easy to print and share, you want pages that are in a PDF format.

STEPS

1. **Click the Advanced Search link to the right of the Search text box, clear the this exact wording or phrase text box, then clear the Search within a site or domain text box**
   English is still selected in the Language list box.

2. **Click in the all these words text box, then type university energy**
   The keywords appear in the Search text box at the top of the form. This text box represents the AND Boolean operator.

3. **Click in the first one or more of these words text box, type alternative, click in the second one or more of these words text box, type sustainable, click in the third one or more of these words text box, then type renewable**
   These text boxes represent the OR Boolean operator. The three words are separated by OR in the Search text box.

4. **Click in the any of these unwanted words text box, then type geothermal**
   This text box represents the NOT Boolean operator, so this keyword appears at the end of the search query as *–geothermal*. Next, you want to filter the results so that only pages in PDF format appear.

5. **Click the File type list arrow, then click Adobe Acrobat PDF (.pdf)**
   Finally, you want to restrict the results to Web pages located in the .ca domain—the domain for Canada.

6. **Click in the Search within a site or domain text box, then type .ca**
   Compare your settings with those shown in Figure B-13. The complete search query is *university energy alternative OR sustainable OR renewable –geothermal filetype:pdf site:.ca* and only English pages were searched.

7. **Click Advanced Search**
   A quick check of the search results verifies that the Boolean text boxes and the filters worked as you expected.

Using the search text boxes on an advanced search page

When using advanced search text boxes, you do not actually type the Boolean operators. When using these specialized text boxes, the search engine understands the operator you want to use, so you can enter multiple words without the operators. However, if you need to enter a phrase in an OR box, you need to include quotation marks around the phrase. For example, to search for *solar panels OR wind turbines* on Google's Advanced Search page, enter: "solar panels" and "wind turbines" in the OR text boxes. This ensures your search is interpreted as two phrases. This is an example of why, when your complex searches get more complicated, as with multiple phrases or more than three keywords separated by OR, it is often preferable to go back to the basic search form.

FIGURE B-13: Using Boolean logic and filters on Google's Advanced Search form

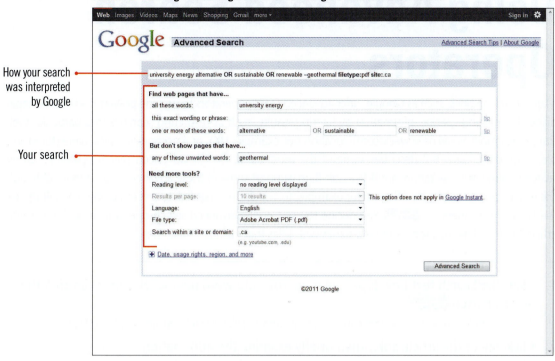

How your search was interpreted by Google

Your search

TABLE B-7: Planning a complex search using both Boolean operators and filters

step	example
1. Identify the first concept. Connect keywords with OR and surround them with parentheses.	(alternative OR renewable OR sustainable)
2. Identify the second concept. Use keywords/synonyms/ related words, connect them with OR, then surround them with parentheses.	(energy OR energies)
3. Identify the third concept.	–geothermal
4. Use filters as needed.	Language: English Domain: .ca File Format: .pdf
5. Create the final search query.	(alternative OR renewable OR sustainable) (energy OR energies) –geothermal site:.ca filetype:.pdf lang:.eng

Using Advanced Search Operators

Major search engines, such as Google, offer advanced search operators to provide powerful additional capabilities for locating specific information by filtering results, such as restricting searches to a particular Web site (for example, www.newsweek.com), location (for example, UK), or a portion of a Web page (for example, page title). Table B-8 describes some of the most useful Google advanced search operators. Other search engines, such as Yahoo! and Microsoft Bing, support some of these advanced search tools, although the exact operator might be different; for example, to search sites that link to a specific domain in Bing, use the LinkDomain operator. You decide to use Google advanced search operators to locate relevant articles in an online magazine and Web pages with titles that include "solar energy."

STEPS

1. **Clear the Search text box, type "solar energy" site:www.newsweek.com, then click the Search button** 🔍

    A list of articles on Newsweek.com containing the phrase *"solar energy"* appears, similar to Figure B-14.

QUICK TIP
For a complete guide to Google advanced search operators, go to googleguide.com/advanced_operators.html.

2. **Click one of the article links, then briefly examine the information**

    After looking at the magazine article, you are ready to search for more Web pages that contain information about solar energy. You decide to search for pages containing *"solar energy"* in the Web page title.

3. **Click the Back button in your browser window to return to your search results on Google**

4. **Clear the Search text box, type allintitle:"solar energy", then click** 🔍

    A list of results appears, as shown in Figure B-15.

5. **Examine the list of results, then click one of the links and read the information on the result Web page**

    The Web page should contain relevant information.

TABLE B-8: Examples of Google Advanced Search operators

operator	allows you to	example
allinanchor:	Locate pages based on the keywords used to link to them from other pages	**allinanchor:useful solar energy sites**—Finds pages that are called useful solar energy sites by other Web sites
allintext:	Locate pages containing all keywords	**allintext:consultant renewable energy**—Finds consultants in renewable energy
allintitle:	Locate pages with titles that contain all keywords	**allintitle:wind power**—Finds pages with titles containing wind power
allinurl:	Locate pages with all keywords appearing in their URLs (Web addresses)	**allinurl:alternative energy**—Finds pages containing alternative energy in the URL
site:	Search a specific Web site based on keywords	**solar energy site:www.newsweek.com**—Finds articles about solar energy on the Newsweek Web site
define:	Locate definitions for words and phrases on the Internet	**define:alternative energy**—Finds definitions for alternative energy
info:	Locate information about a specified page	**info:www.eere.energy.gov**—Finds information about the U.S. Department of Energy Web site
link:	Locate pages that point to a specific URL	**link:www.eere.energy.gov**—Finds pages that link to the U.S. Department of Energy Web site

FIGURE B-14: Search results using Google's *site:* operator

Site: operator in the search query

Results all appear on pages on newsweek.com

Sponsored results are not filtered

FIGURE B-15: Search results using Google's *allintitle:* operator

Allintitle: operator in the search query

Results have *solar energy* in the page title

Sponsored results are not filtered

Using Metasearch Engines

Until now, each of your searches has used a single search engine. Even with complex searching, you only search a single search engine. If one search engine doesn't deliver the number or quality of results you need, or if you want to quickly compare results from different search engines to decide which to use for a particular search, you might want to try a metasearch engine. **Metasearch engines** do not search the Web itself; rather, they search search engines' indexes. By searching more than one search engine's index simultaneously, metasearch engines access more of the Web in a single search. However, metasearch engines often do not search the best search engines, because of the fees such search engines charge. Also, search engines that are busy with too many other searches at the exact moment you conduct your search are sometimes skipped, so results can be inconsistent. Metasearch results are broad, but often not as deep as a single search engine's. Metasearching is a good place to start when you want to check the first few results from several search engines. While searching for information on alternative energy resources, you have become intrigued with geothermal energy. Bob suggests a simple search on this topic using a metasearch engine.

STEPS

1. **Type webcrawler.com in your browser's Address bar, then press [Enter]**
    The WebCrawler search form appears in your browser window.

2. **Click in the Search text box, type "geothermal energy", then click Search**
    Your search is now simultaneously sent to multiple search engines, and the results page appears in your browser window, as shown in Figure B-16. Notice that the search engines that contain each result are listed after the URL for each result, and if the result came from a sponsored result on another search engine, it is labeled as "Ads by." You want to try another metasearch engine.

3. **Type yippy.com in your browser's Address bar, then press [Enter]**
    The Yippy search form appears in your browser window.

4. **Click in the Search text box, type "geothermal energy", then click Search**
    The results appear in the browser window, similar to those shown in Figure B-17. Note each Yippy search result contains a brief description of the item found, its URL, and the sources the item came from, including search engines and directories. In addition, at the top of the results, Yippy displays a definition of the search term, which is drawn from the online research library HighBeam. Yippy also groups search results into useful categories called clouds in the upper-left corner of the results page. Clicking a cloud causes Yippy to show search results for just that category.

5. **Click the Green link in the list of clouds**
    Many fewer results are displayed because only results in the Green category are now listed. Note that this is not the same as adding *green* as a term in the search query.

Maximizing metasearching

To effectively use a metasearch engine, always read its Help pages to determine how "smart" the engine is in translating specific search commands into queries that other search engines understand. With this information, you can learn if you need to use quotation marks to indicate a phrase. If you're not sure how smart the metasearch engine is, use simple searches consisting of only a few keywords. Also, because the search engines used by a metasearch engine change regularly, note which engines are being used when you perform your search and which are returning the most useful results.

FIGURE B-16: Search results for *"geothermal energy"* in WebCrawler

Your search query

Search engines on which result was indexed

Suggested alternative searches

Sponsored result from Yahoo!

FIGURE B-17: Search results for *"geothermal energy"* in Yippy

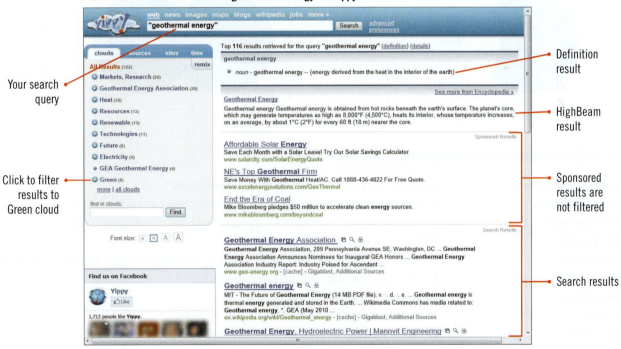

Your search query

Click to filter results to Green cloud

Definition result

HighBeam result

Sponsored results are not filtered

Search results

Practice

For current SAM information, including versions and content details, visit SAM Central (http://www.cengage.com/samcentral). If you have a SAM user profile, you may have access to hands-on instruction, practice, and assessment of the skills covered in this unit. Since various versions of SAM are supported throughout the life of this text, check with your instructor for the correct instructions and URL/Web site for accessing assignments.

Concepts Review

Each of the following Venn diagrams represents searches. The blue color represents the search results. Write out the search for each diagram.

FIGURE B-18

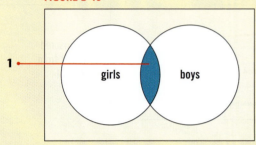

1

FIGURE B-19

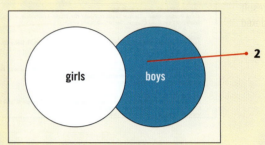

2

FIGURE B-20

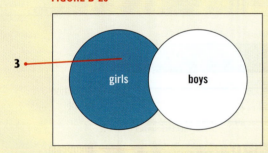

3

FIGURE B-21

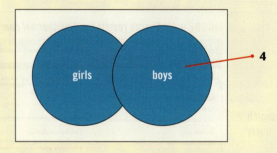

4

Match each term with the statement that best describes it.

5. **Boolean operators**
6. **Venn diagrams**
7. **AND operator**
8. **OR operator**
9. **NOT operator**
10. **Metasearch engine**
11. **Parentheses**
12. **Filters**
13. **Algorithm**

a. A way to visualize how Boolean operators work
b. Indicate how keywords are to relate to each other in a search query
c. A mathematical formula used by search engines to rank search results
d. Used to exclude words from a search query
e. A search engine that searches multiple search engines rather than the Web itself
f. Aids to screen out unwanted Web pages
g. One way to narrow a search
h. Used to connect synonyms
i. Force the order of operation in a Boolean search

Select the best answer from the list of choices.

14. The place where two search results sets overlap is called the _____ of the two sets.
    a. union
    b. intersection
    c. margin
    d. combination

15. When you use the Boolean operator AND to link another keyword to your search query, you find:
    a. exactly the same number of Web pages.
    b. more Web pages.
    c. fewer Web pages.
    d. None of the above.

16. Equivalent wording for the Boolean OR in an advanced search list box might be:
    a. must not contain.
    b. all of the words.
    c. either of the words.
    d. none of the words.

17. Which is not a standard variation of the Boolean operator NOT?
    a. AND NOT
    b. ANDNOT
    c. The hyphen or minus sign (–)
    d. NOT MORE

18. Which is not a potential downside to using metasearch engines?
    a. Usually limited to simple searches
    b. Don't search the best search engines
    c. Inconsistency
    d. Instability

19. If the order of operation in a complex Boolean search is not forced, the search tool:
    a. automatically applies filters to your search.
    b. reads the query from left to right.
    c. inserts the parentheses for you.
    d. returns no search results.

20. A search tool that doesn't recognize Boolean operators as English words in its basic search:
    a. cannot be used to search with Boolean logic.
    b. sometimes allows the Boolean AND and NOT if you use the plus sign (+) and the minus sign (–) instead of words.
    c. probably allows Boolean searching from text boxes or list boxes in its advanced search pages.
    d. b and c

21. The part of a URL that can contain a two-letter country code is the:
    a. domain.
    b. page.
    c. file extension.
    d. file.

22. Which is *not* true of metasearch engines?
    a. They search other search engines' indexes.
    b. They might skip searching an engine they normally search if that engine is busy at that moment.
    c. They are a good place to start when you want to see the top results from several engines.
    d. Their results are always as deep as individual search engines.

23. **Using parentheses in a complex search tells the search engine that:**
  a. the words inside the parentheses should be treated as a subset in the search.
  b. the part of the search inside the parentheses should be performed first.
  c. the words inside the parentheses should be excluded from the search.
  d. a and b

Skills Review

If requested by your instructor, create a document listing the answers to the questions asked in the following exercises.

1. **Understand Boolean operators.**
  a. Describe the effects on search results when you use the Boolean operator AND.
  b. Describe the effects on search results when you use the Boolean operator OR.
  c. Describe the effects on search results when you use the Boolean operator NOT.
  d. What symbol can you use instead of the Boolean operator AND?
  e. What symbol can you use instead of the Boolean operator NOT?

2. **Narrow a search with the AND operator.**
  a. Go to the Google basic search form.
  b. Perform an initial search on **energy**, and note the number of results.
  c. Edit your search query by adding **green** to it, run the search, and then note the number of results.
  d. Modify your search query again by adding **solutions**. Run the search, and then note the number of results.
  e. How did the number of results change after each search (in other words, did the number increase or decrease)? Why?

3. **Expand a search with the OR operator.**
  a. Return to your initial search for **energy**.
  b. Modify your search query by adding **OR renewable**, run the search, and then note the number of results.
  c. Modify your search query again by adding **OR technologies**, run the search, and then note the number of results.
  d. How did adding each OR statement affect the number of results? Why?

4. **Restrict a search with the NOT operator.**
  a. Return to your initial search for **energy**.
  b. Modify your search query by adding **–renewable**, run the search, and then note the number of results.
  c. Modify your search query again by adding **–technologies**, run the search, and then note the number of results.
  d. How did adding each NOT statement affect the number of results? Why?

5. **Use multiple Boolean operators.**
  a. Clear the Google Search text box, and then perform a search using the search query **energy green OR renewable**. Note the number of results.
  b. Clear the Google Search text box, and then retype the search query from step a, but this time enclose **green OR renewable** in parentheses. Run the search again. Note the number of results.
  c. How did adding the parentheses affect the number of results?
  d. Clear the Google Search text box, and then retype the search query from step b, but modify it by adding **(solutions OR technologies)** to the search criteria. Run the search, and then note the number of results.
  e. How did adding each of the multiple Boolean operators affect the number of results? Why?

Skills Review (continued)

6. **Search with filters.**

   a. Clear the Google Search text box, and then click the Advanced search link, and clear the text boxes on the page of any search criteria.

   b. Enter text in the appropriate text box or boxes on the Advanced Search page to create the search query **energy green OR renewable**.

   c. Run the search, and note the number of search results.

   d. Return to the Advanced Search page, and then add a filter for Web pages written in English, a filter for Web pages modified and indexed in the past year, and a filter for pages with the domain **.org**.

   e. Run the search, and note the number of search results.

   f. What was the final search query (including any labels that identify the filters applied)?

7. **Combine Boolean operators and filters.**

   a. Clear the Google Advanced Search text boxes and filters.

   b. Enter text in the appropriate text box or boxes on the Advanced Search page to create the search query **energy efficient renewable**.

   c. Enter text in the appropriate text box or boxes on the Advanced Search page to add the search phrase **"department of energy"** to the search query.

   d. Run the search, and note the number of search results.

   e. Return to the Advanced Search page, and then add a filter for Web pages written in English, a filter for pages modified and indexed in the past year, and a filter for pages with the domain **.net**.

   f. Run the search, and note the number of search results.

   g. What was the final search query (including any labels that identify the filters applied)?

8. **Use advanced search operators.**

   a. Go to the Google basic search form.

   b. Create a search query using the appropriate advanced search operator to search for **renewable energy** only on the Web www.time.com.

   c. Run the search. If requested by your instructor, print or save this page of results.

   d. Explore one of the articles at the Time magazine site.

   e. Return to the Google search page, and then clear the Search text box.

   f. Create a search query using the appropriate advanced search operator to find Web pages that have the exact phrase **"renewable energy"** in the page title.

   g. Run the search. If requested by your instructor, print or save this page of results.

   h. Explore one of the links to see if the result is relevant.

9. **Use metasearch engines.**

   a. Go to the WebCrawler metasearch engine at **webcrawler.com**.

   b. Perform an initial search using the search query **"green energy"**. If requested by your instructor, print or save this page of results.

   c. Go to the Yippy metasearch engine at **yippy.com**.

   d. Repeat the search at this Web site. Note the number of results. If requested by your instructor, print or save this page of results.

   e. Filter the search to include only results in the Wind cloud. (If you don't see a Wind cloud, click another cloud.) Note the number of results. If requested by your instructor, print or save this page of results.

Independent Challenge 1

If requested by your instructor, create a document listing the answer to the question asked in the following exercises.

You want to find Web sites in Spain (domain .es) about the Picasso Museum in Barcelona. You don't read Spanish, so you want the Web pages to be in English.

    a. Use the Google Advanced Search page to set the appropriate filters, and then perform your search.

    b. Modify the search query to include only Web pages in PDF format.

    c. Run the search again. Examine the search results.

    d. Go to the Yippy metasearch engine at **yippy.com**. Click Search (without typing anything in the Search text box), and then click the advanced link next to the Search text box. Repeat the search using the Yippy Advanced Search form. Compare the results with the results you received when you used Google. Are any of the results on the first page of results from Yippy the same as the results on the first page of results from Google?

Independent Challenge 2

If requested by your instructor, create a document listing the answers to the questions asked in the following exercises.

You need to find something to help you create a personal budget. You want to consider both software and tools that you can fill out by hand.

    a. Go to the Google basic search form, create a search query, and then perform your search.

    b. Scroll through the first page of results.

    c. In the pane on the left, click the Related searches link, and then click one of the related links that appears at the top of the results. Examine the first page in this set of results. Which set of results seems to be more relevant?

Advanced Challenge Exercise

    ■ Go to the WebCrawler metasearch engine at **webcrawler.com**. Select whichever search yielded the best results, conduct that search, and then examine the results. Are they the same as the Google results?

    ■ Go to the MetaCrawler metasearch engine at **metacrawler.com**. Conduct the same search, and then examine these results. Are they similar to the results WebCrawler returned? How do they compare to Google?

    ■ Go to the Dogpile metasearch engine at **dogpile.com**, and then perform the same search. Once again, examine the results and compare them to the Google, WebCrawler, and MetaCrawler results.

    ■ Which metasearch engine do you think returned the most relevant results?

Independent Challenge 3

If requested by your instructor, create a document listing the answers to the questions asked in the following exercises.

You and some friends want to go on an ecotour (an ecologically friendly vacation). You are interested in tours to Central and South America, but you need the information to be in English.

    a. Consider your search query, and think of synonyms and related words.

    b. Construct a search query, and then run the search using the Google basic search form.

    c. Modify your search query by adding multiple Boolean operators and using parentheses to look for ecotours that include volunteer work or community development as part of the tour. What is your final search query?

    d. Examine your results, and then identify a Web site that seems to have tours that meet your needs. Run a new search that searches for pages with links that point to the Web site you identified. (*Hint*: Use the link: operator.) What is your final search query?

Independent Challenge 3 (continued)

Advanced Challenge Exercise

You want to find an ecotour in Costa Rica or Patagonia that focuses on the rainforest or wildlife. You decide to restrict your search to find only relevant sites in English.

- Go to the Google Basic Search page, and then type a complex search query in the Search text box. Run the search, and then examine your results. Modify the query as needed to get relevant results.
- Open a new tab or browser window, go to the Google Advanced Search page, and then try to use the form to create your search query. Run the search, and then examine your results.
- Which search, the basic or the advanced, provided the best results?
- Was it easier to construct your specific search query using the basic or the advanced search form?

Real Life Independent Challenge

If requested by your instructor, create a document listing the answers to the questions asked in the following exercises.

In our increasingly long-lived society, the number of career changes over a lifetime continues to grow. Fortunately, the Internet provides a wealth of information on how to choose a career, with everything from career-path quizzes to professional advice. You decide to avail yourself of these resources to find out how to chart a career.

a. Conduct a search on Google using the search query **choose career**. Examine the results.
b. Broaden your search by adding multiple Boolean operators so that the search query includes the following synonyms for the word *choose*: *pick*, *select*, and *find*. (*Hint*: Make sure you use the Boolean operator that broadens your results, not narrows them.) Examine your results.
c. Modify your search query again to exclude career quizzes and tests from the results (because you are looking for advice only). Examine your results.
d. Modify your search again so that the results include pages that are specific to a career that you are interested in. Examine your results.

Visual Workshop

Construct a search query on Bing using the basic search form to find the Web page shown in Figure B-22. This page is stored on the NASA Web site. Your query should be precise enough so this page is one of the first few results. If requested by your instructor, print or save the page on which this photo is displayed.

FIGURE B-22

STS-134 Shuttle Mission Imagery

S134-E-010137 (29 May 2011) --- The International Space Station is featured in this image photographed by an STS-134 crew member on the space shuttle Endeavour after the station and shuttle began their post-undocking relative separation. Undocking of the two spacecraft occurred at 11:55 p.m. (EDT) on May 29, 2011. Endeavour spent 11 days, 17 hours and 41 minutes attached to the orbiting laboratory. Photo credit: NASA

high res (1.3 M) low res (90 K)

Curator: Kim Dismukes | Responsible NASA Official: Amiko Kauderer | Updated: 05/30/2011
Web Accessibility and Policy Notices

UNIT C
Internet Research

Finding Specialty Information

You have already learned to use search engines for general research. Sometimes, however, you are unfamiliar with a field and need to garner an overview of it. To do this, you can use Web sites organized into topics and subtopics. Other times the information you want is very specific, such as someone's name, the address of a business, or the definition of a word. This kind of specialty information is often stored in online databases that require direct access, making traditional search engines ineffective. You can find specialty information through specialty Web sites that include online telephone directories, maps, periodicals, and government sites. Fortunately, specialty search engines make it easier to locate the information stored in many of these Web databases. You will be attending a conference on renewable energy in Washington, D.C. In preparing for this conference, you speak with Bob Johnson, the reference librarian, who suggests you continue your research on alternative energy using specialty search engines and subject directories.

OBJECTIVES

Understand subject guides

Use a subject guide

Understand the deep Web

Search periodical databases

Find places

Find people and businesses

Use a specialized search engine

Find online reference sources

Find government information

Understanding Subject Guides

Subject guides, also known as **subject directories**, **Internet directories**, and **subject trees**, are indexed Web pages that are usually compiled by hand and maintained by people, and that are organized into alphabetical and hierarchical topics. The people are often either experts in the field they are indexing or research professionals, such as librarians. Carefully designed selection criteria are used to select resources to include in subject guides. This offers users greater selectivity and quality of information but less coverage than search engines. Some subject guides now provide search engines, and some search engines provide subject guides. Most subject guides' engines still search only their hand-selected indexes, and most of the subject categories in a search engine's subject guide are still compiled electronically from all sites crawled by their spiders. Table C-1 lists several subject guides. You want to become more efficient at searching the Web for reliable information on alternative energy, so you decide to learn more about subject guides.

DETAILS

Figures C-1 and C-2 illustrate the following notable characteristics of subject guides:

- **Organization**

  Subject guides organize links to Web sites into topical hierarchies. A **hierarchy** is a ranked order. The ranked order typically goes from more general to more specific. For example, the general topics or categories (in bold) in the Open Directory Project subject guide, shown in Figure C-1, are followed by related, more specific topics, or subcategories. Clicking a topic, such as Science, links to a list of subtopics. Subtopics link to increasingly detailed topics. You navigate or browse a subject guide primarily by "**drilling down**," or clicking through topics and subtopics arranged hierarchically, under increasingly specific subject headings.

- **Selectivity**

  Subject guides are selective. In better subject guides, qualified people rather than computer programs decide which Web pages are worthy of inclusion. Subject guides can provide links to useful sites that search engine spiders are unable to access. They often include Web pages with links to other sites covering all aspects of a topic. Subject experts also include sites that might cover one or two very detailed subtopics. This kind of selectivity ensures that returned Web pages are some of the best on the subject. Because of this selectivity, subject guides are relatively small, which can be an advantage, saving you the time and trouble of sifting through thousands of search engine results.

- **Accessibility**

  In addition to hierarchical lists of topics, better subject guides provide search forms with which you can use keywords to search the indexed Web pages. A subject guide might also provide its lists of topics arranged in multiple ways, such as listing topics alphabetically, geographically, chronologically, or by the Dewey Decimal subject classification system.

QUICK TIP

Annotations are great time-savers, as they provide expert previews of sites for you.

- **Annotations**

  Annotations are summaries or reviews of the contents of a Web page, written by the subject guide contributors, usually experts in the field, such as professionals or academics, or experts in information and the Web, such as librarians. Annotations make subject guides the tools of choice for many researchers.

- **Relevant results**

  Subject guides return fewer results than search engines, but the results are more likely to be reliable and useful. As shown in Figure C-2, typical subject guide results pages include the number of results, an annotation for each result, and topics under which related sites are indexed. The latter can be especially useful when you are just beginning to learn about your topic and how it relates to other subjects.

FIGURE C-1: Open Directory Project home page

Search text box

Alphabetically and hierarchically arranged subject categories and subcategories

Link to Help information

Click to open advanced search form

Subject categories

Subject subcategories

FIGURE C-2: Search results for renewable energy on the Open Directory Project

Your search query

Categories and subcategories under which the results are organized

Number of results

Link to a result

URL of a result

Identifies the number of results in this category; click to restrict the search to this category

Click to see additional categories that contain the results

Annotations

Link to the category under which result is categorized

TABLE C-1: Sampling of subject guides

subject guide	URL	type	features
EERE	eere.energy.gov	Government energy specific	Searchable
INFOMINE	infomine.ucr.edu	Academic/scholarly/distributed	Searchable, created by librarians, high quality
ipl2	ipl2.org	General/reference	Searchable, created by librarians, university-based, high quality
Open Directory Project	dmoz.org	General/distributed	Largest human-edited directory, maintained by volunteer editors from all over the world who need to apply and be accepted as an expert
Scout Archives	scout.wisc.edu/Archives	Academic/reference	Searchable, university-based, high quality
WWW Virtual Library	vlib.org	Academic/general/distributed	First subject guide on the Web

Finding Specialty Information

Using a Subject Guide

Each subject guide has a unique way of organizing information. Links relating to "Energy" might appear under "Science" at one guide and under "Technology" at another. By clicking your way through the hierarchy of topics, from the most general to the most specific, you see which sites were deemed best by the guide's contributors. You can also search using keywords, and if you are unsure of keywords when starting your research, browsing a subject guide can help you identify effective ones to use. 🖌 You decide to continue your search for information about alternative energy by browsing a few subject guides. You start with the Scout Archives.

STEPS

QUICK TIP
The Scout Archives subject directory was created in 1994 and is maintained by the University of Wisconsin.

1. **Start your browser, type scout.wisc.edu/archives in your browser's Address bar, then press [Enter]**
   You have options for a keyword search, an advanced search, or browsing through subject headings.

2. **Under Browse by Library of Congress Subject Headings, click the letter R**
   A list of categories starting with the letter *R* appears.

3. **Click the Renewable energy sources link**
   Your results appear, and above the list of indexed pages are several classifications or subcategories to further focus your results.

QUICK TIP
If the path you drill down doesn't yield the results you need, navigate back and try another path.

4. **Click the United States link under Classifications**
   See Figure C-3. Now you decide to use *renewable energy* as keywords for a search.

5. **Click in the Search Archives text box, type renewable energy, then click GO**
   You decide to examine a full record of one of the results.

6. **Click the Full Record link for one of the results**
   Your results should look similar to Figure C-4.

Understanding distributed subject guides

WWW Virtual Library and the Open Directory Project are examples of distributed subject guides. Some subject guides are maintained in one location by individuals or organizations. Others, called **distributed subject guides**, are created by a variety of contributors who work somewhat independently on a subtopic of a main topic and are maintained on more than one computer. These guides are said to be "distributed" because rather than being on one computer, the Web pages for different parts of the guide are stored on different computers, which are distributed around the country or around the world. Because distributed subject guides have many contributors working independently, each with varying levels of expertise and resources, distributed subject guides tend to have an uneven quality and a lack of standardization. However, this potential downside is balanced by the fact that these different parts of the guide's index are usually maintained by subject experts with a high level of awareness of what is available on the Web in their field. Note that in a distributed subject guide, clicking categories might direct your browser to a site on a different Web server.

FIGURE C-3: Drill-down results through Renewable energy sources/United States on the Scout Archives

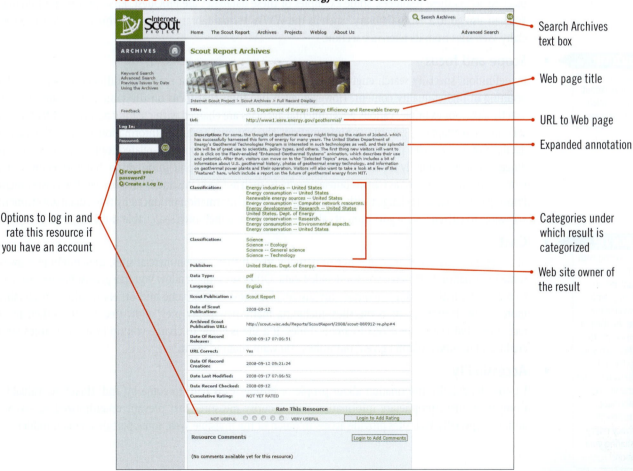

Search Archives text box for keyword search

Advanced Search link

Information about Internet Scout Project is on the home page

Drill-down path

Options for drilling down further to subcategories

Annotation

Drill-down results

URL to result

Link to full record on the Scout Report Archives

Date annotated result was last updated (not necessarily the date the Web page was last updated)

FIGURE C-4: Search results for *renewable energy* on the Scout Archives

Search Archives text box

Web page title

URL to Web page

Expanded annotation

Options to log in and rate this resource if you have an account

Categories under which result is categorized

Web site owner of the result

Finding Specialty Information

Understanding the Deep Web

By far, the largest part of the Internet is hidden from most search tools. As you learned in Unit A, this hidden content is called the **deep Web** or the **invisible Web**. The search engines you have used so far search for information on the **surface Web** or **visible Web**, which is the portion of the Web indexed by traditional search engine spiders. Deep Web content largely resides in online databases and is unavailable to traditional search engines because these databases require direct queries at their sites. Common examples are online phone books or newspaper and magazine archives. Other examples include **dynamically generated Web pages**, which are Web pages that databases create based on specific queries or pages that require a login name and password. Figure C-5 provides a conceptual view of Internet content searched by traditional search engines contrasted with the content searched by specialty search tools. Not wanting to ignore a large part of the information available via the Internet, you decide to learn about research tools that can help make the invisible Web accessible.

DETAILS

The following are important points to remember when using specialty search tools:

- **Specialty information**

  Typically, you locate hidden Web content by going to a specialty Web site and using its search form to query a database. Although much of the invisible Web is available publicly, some specialized databases require subscriptions. Because libraries pay the subscription fees for many of these specialty sites, they are a good place to access these resources. Some examples of these databases are ProQuest, EBSCOhost, and InfoTrac. You can also go to a "virtual library" such as the WWW Virtual Library (vlib.org), which links to these specialty Web sites from its reference section.

- **Scope and focus**

  By definition, specialty search engines and directories tend to have a narrower and deeper focus, usually resulting in higher-quality content. However, even two tools that focus on the same narrow area are not exactly alike. For example, various governmental agencies are charged with creating access to different, but sometimes overlapping, government information. The National Technical Information Service (NTIS) has a database of government publications on scientific, technical, and business-related topics. The U.S. Census Bureau database primarily focuses on Web sites containing demographic information, but also features data related to business, as well as Census Bureau products, such as CD-ROMs and DVDs for sale. The Government Printing Office (GPO) is charged with making much of the information produced by the federal government accessible to citizens. State governments also usually provide their own searchable sites.

- **Cost**

  Most specialty Web sites are either free or partially free. If they are commercial sites, they might give away some information but charge you for detailed data. Other sites might allow you free access, but require you to register with them—some require only an email address or username and others require considerably more personal information. Some sites, including many newspaper sites, allow free access to their most recent files but charge for access to archival files. If a site is going to charge you up front, it requires your credit card number, so don't give it out unless you want them to use it.

- **Accessibility**

  Up-to-date, detailed information about people or businesses is hard to come by and, therefore, valuable. Companies guard proprietary information with security measures that prevent unauthorized access. So, although specialty Web sites provide access to much of the invisible Web, some portions remain hidden.

FIGURE C-5: Internet content searched by traditional search tools contrasted with content searched by specialty search tools*

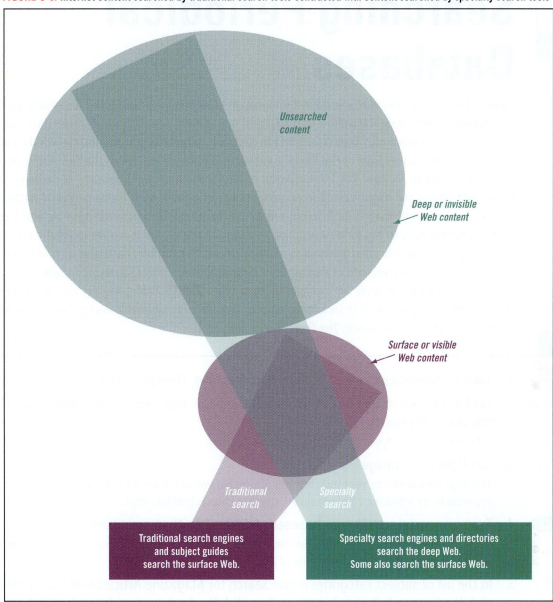

Unsearched content

Deep or invisible Web content

Surface or visible Web content

Traditional search

Specialty search

Traditional search engines and subject guides search the surface Web.

Specialty search engines and directories search the deep Web. Some also search the surface Web.

* Conceptual only. If this figure were to scale, the deep Web portion would be dozens of times larger than the surface Web.

Comparing the visible and invisible Web

It is impossible to know the exact size of the invisible or deep Web; however, a conservative estimate places it at approximately 500 times larger than the visible or surface Web. Since the surface Web has more than a trillion pages, the deep Web is likely more than 500 trillion pages in size. In other words, about 99.8 percent of the information on the Web is largely hidden from the view of traditional search engines.

Internet Research

Searching Periodical Databases

Some of the most authoritative and current information hidden in the invisible Web is stored in **periodical databases**. These include the archives of magazines, newspapers, and scholarly journals. Some sites on the Web are "online newsstands." They collect links to electronic periodicals from around the world on all topics. Some periodicals, such as *Salon* or *First Monday*, exist only in electronic format on the Web. Other periodicals, such as *The Times* or *The New York Times*, have an online version that might not carry all the same stories as the printed version and might include some stories not seen in print. Most online periodical databases provide limited recent information for free, but require payment for older, archived materials, and some have started requiring users to pay for a subscription to access all articles. Some require registration but may ask you to log in only after reading a certain number of articles. Subscription databases such as ProQuest and InfoTrac store electronic versions of thousands of periodical titles. Table C-2 describes differences between types of periodicals and gives an example of each type. Before leaving for the conference in Washington, D.C., you decide to look for some current articles on renewable energy topics to read on the plane. You begin your search with *The Times*.

STEPS

TROUBLE

If your search did not find any articles, try another search using another alternative energy topic. If your search still does not yield any articles, enter any other keywords.

1. **Type thetimes.co.uk in your browser's Address Bar, then press [Enter]**

2. **Click in the Search text box at the top of the page, type renewable energy, then click the Search button** 🔍

   Your search results appear, listing links to relevant articles.

3. **Scroll the results page**

   This page sorts results by relevancy, but you notice that you also have the option of sorting by date. Next, you want to try searching a periodical database that indexes multiple titles.

QUICK TIP

When you use periodical databases, you might encounter some articles that are available to subscribers only. Your librarian can usually get these articles for you.

4. **Type magportal.com in your browser's Address bar, then press [Enter]**

   MagPortal offers broad topical categories you can navigate by drilling down to find articles of interest as well as a search engine for keyword searching of the database.

5. **In the list of subject categories in the Search for Magazine Articles text box on the right, click the Science & Technology link, then click the Environment & Geology link in the list of subcategories**

   Figure C-6 shows results from drilling down through the subject categories. A Search Articles text box is also available on the results page. The all articles option button is selected by default below the Search Articles text box.

6. **Click in the Search Articles text box, type renewable energy, then click Search**

   Figure C-7 shows the search results page. The small wavy line icon at the end of each article links you to similar articles. You notice that you can sort your results several ways. The results are currently sorted by quality of match, as shown in the order by list box.

QUICK TIP

Note the annotations, which can help you quickly identify which articles might be most useful.

7. **Click the order by list arrow near the top of the page, click date, then click Search**

   The results are re-sorted and appear in order of date published, with the most recently published articles appearing first.

FIGURE C-6: MagPortal subject categories results

Search Articles text box

Subject categories

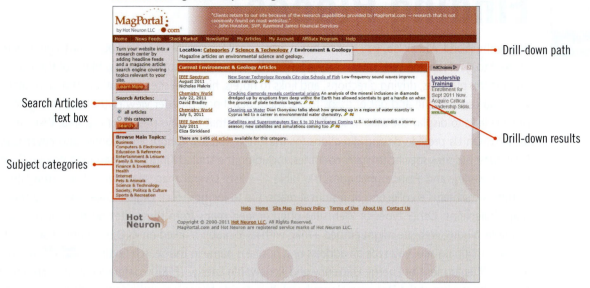

Drill-down path

Drill-down results

FIGURE C-7: MagPortal search results

Your search query

Suggestions for related categories

Search results

Click to change result sort order

Click for similar articles

TABLE C-2: Periodicals and their distinguishing characteristics

periodical type	purpose	publisher	audience	documentation	example
Scholarly/research	Original research/experiments	University/organization	Scholars/professionals/university students	Citations/bibliography	*Harvard Educational Review*
Professional/special interest	Professional practice/case studies	Organization	Professionals/university students	May cite or provide bibliography	*Journal of Accountancy*
General interest	Inform/entertain	Commercial	Knowledgeable reader/possibly technical	May mention sources	*The New York Times*
Popular	Entertain	Commercial	General audience/simple language	Rarely mentions sources	*People Magazine*

Finding Places

Before the World Wide Web, you had to buy a map or call for directions to find out how to get where you wanted to go. Now the Web offers quite a few good map and locator Web sites. Many of these sites also provide trip planners, driving directions, and links to hotels, historical sites, and other attractions along the way. You can zoom in and out of maps to see more detail or a broader view of the area. Many sites also provide links to display the map in satellite view or a view that displays photos of the area. Web sites such as Maps On Us provide driving directions for the United States. Yahoo! and Google also cover Canada. MapQuest has sites specific to many countries, including the United Kingdom (mapquest.co.uk), Germany (mapquest.de), and France (mapquest.fr). Table C-3 lists several map sites. In addition, the Library of Congress maintains a collection of historical maps. Go to loc.gov, click Digital Collections, and then click Map Collections. Other types of Web sites often embed maps from these sites on their own pages; for example, a hotel Web site might embed a map with its location marked on its Directions or Location page. To use a mapping site, you type an address or a business name in the Search text box. You plan to attend a Department of Energy Efficiency and Renewable Energy (EERE) conference in Washington, D.C. You will be staying at the Donovan House hotel. You decide to use a mapping site to find its location.

STEPS

1. **Type maps.google.com in your browser's Address bar, then press [Enter]**

   The Google Maps home page opens. It might show a map of the entire United States, your local area, or another local area.

   > **QUICK TIP**
   > If the map looks like the view from a satellite instead of Figure C-8, click the Maps button in the upper-right corner of the map.

2. **Click in the Search text box, type Donovan House, Washington, DC, then click the Search Maps button** 🔍

   A map of the Washington, D.C., area appears with the Donovan House identified on the map. See Figure C-8.

3. **Click the Zoom In button ⊕ on the map three times**

   The map zooms in so you can clearly see that the Donovan House is located on 14th Street Northwest, near Thomas Circle Park.

   > **TROUBLE**
   > If the image is showing the street from a different position, drag across the image from left to right as many times as needed until the image approximately matches Figure C-9.

4. **Drag the person icon at the top of the Zoom bar onto the map to display blue lines, then release the mouse button when the green icon at the person's feet is pointing to the Donovan House location**

   Street view, which is a series of photos of the area, appears in place of the map. See Figure C-9. If blue lines do not appear when you drag the person icon onto a map, then Street view is not available for that street.

5. **Click the Exit street view button ⊠ in the top right corner of the map, then click the Satellite button**

   The view from a satellite appears with the map overlaid on the image, and the Satellite button changes to the Map button.

6. **Click ⊞ as many times as necessary to zoom in all the way, point to Traffic under the Map button to display the list of commands, then click Labels to deselect it**

   You see a close-up view of the area from a satellite without street labels.

   > **QUICK TIP**
   > Click Traffic again to toggle the colored lines off.

7. **Point to Traffic, click Traffic, then click the Zoom Out button ⊟ one time**

   A check mark appears next to Traffic, and colored lines appear on the roads in the map. Green indicates that traffic is flowing at a normal pace, yellow indicates that there is moderately heavy traffic and it is moving a little slower than normal, and red indicates that traffic is very heavy and is moving very slowly.

8. **Click the Donovan House link next to the letter *A* in the left pane**

   A page displaying the name of the business, its address, phone number, links to its Website, and other helpful information appears with a smaller version of the map.

FIGURE C-8: Map of Washington, D.C., area with Donovan House identified

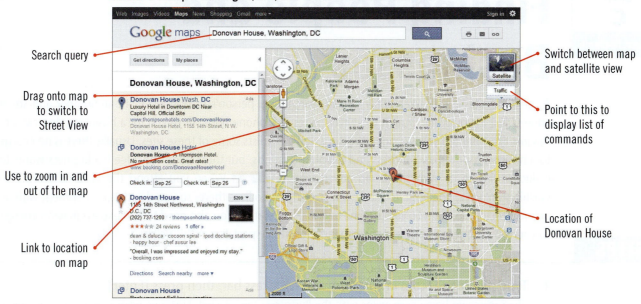

Search query

Switch between map and satellite view

Drag onto map to switch to Street View

Point to this to display list of commands

Use to zoom in and out of the map

Location of Donovan House

Link to location on map

FIGURE C-9: Street view of 14th St. NW in front of the Donovan House hotel

Click to exit Street View

Yellow and white lines indicate routes along which images were taken

Click to advance Street View to the next photo in the direction indicated by the yellow and white lines

TABLE C-3: Mapping Web sites

Web site	URL	features
Google Maps	maps.google.com	Traffic updates, satellite view, street photos, walking directions, public transit directions, bicycling directions
Bing Maps	bing.com/maps	Traffic updates, satellite view, photos from the air, street photos, walking directions, public transit information
MapQuest	mapquest.com	Traffic updates, satellite view, street photos
Maps on Us	mapsonus.com	Traffic updates, satellite photos, walking directions
Streetmap	streetmap.co.uk	Lists businesses in the area
Rand McNally Travel Store	maps.randmcnally.com	Lists businesses in the area, videos of sites in area
Yahoo! Maps	maps.yahoo.com	Traffic updates, satellite view

Finding People and Businesses

A variety of sites on the Web allow you to search for a person's or business's phone number and street address just as you would search the white pages of a phone book, or search for a business using categories just like a printed yellow pages directory. Table C-4 lists some of these sites. Usually, there is no charge to a business for the basic address and telephone listings, but there might be a fee if a business wants to include a link to its Web site or an advertisement.  When you attend the EERE conference in Washington, D.C., you hope to meet with a relative who lives there, so you decide to experiment with an online directory so that you can use one to find your relative. You also need to find experts in wind energy, so you will search for businesses and organizations that specialize in this field.

STEPS

1. **Type superpages.com in your browser's Address bar, then press [Enter]**

   The Superpages home page opens with the Businesses tab selected. First, you want to look for someone in your city or town who shares your name.

2. **Click the People tab**

   See Figure C-10. The People tab appears with options for looking for information about people.

> **TROUBLE**
> Many sites include sponsored results and links for advanced searches that require you to pay a fee.

3. **In the bar at the top of the page, click in the First Name text box, type your first initial, click in the Last Name text box, type your last name, click in the Location text box, type your city and state, then click Search**

   A list of names appears. Directory searches often provide better results using just an initial, rather than a first name. Notice the Map and Driving Directions links under each result. Most directories that list white and yellow pages results include links to a mapping site, allowing you to jump instantly to a map of the location where the person or business is located.

4. **Click your name or another name in the list or results**

   A new page opens with data for the person whose name you clicked. Now you want to find businesses and organizations in the field of wind energy in the Washington, D.C., area.

> **QUICK TIP**
> You can also use map sites to locate information about businesses.

5. **Click the Businesses tab**

   You need to specify the city for you search first.

6. **Click the select location or change link on the right edge of the bar at the top of the page to display a list of large cities in the United States, then click Washington, DC**

7. **Click in the Search text box, type wind energy, then click Search**

   A list of results appears, along with options to narrow the search to businesses within a certain distance of a zip code or to change the category. See Figure C-11.

8. **Click the Wind Energy Systems link under Category in the left pane**

   The list is narrowed to display only companies that sell wind energy systems.

Finding personal email addresses and telephone numbers

Some white pages sites search for email addresses, but, largely due to spamming, most people no longer want their email addresses available to spiders on the Web. Also, email addresses tend to change frequently, even for professional or commercial sites, so addresses found through searches might be out of date. Telephone numbers can also be difficult to find for those who have opted out of being listed in telephone directories.

FIGURE C-10: People tab on Superpages

People tab

First Name text box

Last Name text box

Location text box

FIGURE C-11: WhitePagesSearch results in the Wind Energy category in Washington, D.C., on the Business tab on Superpages

Click to change city

Category in Search text box

Options to narrow results

Results of search

Map of area with results labeled

TABLE C-4: Features of selected business finder Web sites

Web site	country	white pages	yellow pages	maps
AnyWho.com	US	X	X	X
Canada411.ca	Canada	X	X	
Europages.com	Europe		X	
Scoot.co.uk	UK		X	X
Superpages.com	US	X	X	X
UKphonebook.com	UK	X	X	
Whitepages.com	US	X	X	
Yell.com	UK		X	
Yellowpages.ca	Canada	X	X	X
Yellowpages.com.au	Australia	X	X	X

Internet Research

Using a Specialized Search Engine

Specialized search engines are similar to regular Web search engines, except, like some subject guides, they limit the Web pages they search by subject. Specialized search engines are available for a wide variety of topics, including law, medicine, computers, and energy. For example, SearchEdu.com searches school and university sites only. The specialized search engine Scirus is a search engine that indexes only science-specific information on the Internet. You decide to use this specialized search engine to search for information about biomass wind energy.

TROUBLE
As of the date this book was published, these steps were accurate. However, this Web site might change during the lifetime of this book. If an error message appears instead of the Web site's home page, try using a basic search engine to search for SciVerse.

1. **Type scirus.com in your browser's Address bar, then press [Enter]**
   The site's home page appears. You can conduct a search from the home page, or, as with ordinary search engines, you can use the site's Advanced search page.

2. **Click the Advanced search link**
   The Advanced search page appears, as shown in Figure C-12. Notice that All of the words and the Boolean operator AND are the default selections for creating a search phrase.

3. **Click in the first Search text box next to All of the words, type "wind energy", click in the second Search text box next to the second All of the words, then type biomass**
   Now you will specify that only recent results should be returned. The default is to return results published before 1900 through the current year.

4. **Click the before 1900 list arrow in the Dates section, then click the year two years prior to the current year**
   You only want to see results that are Web pages.

5. **Click the HTML check box in the File formats section**
   The HTML check box is selected and the Any format check box is automatically deselected. Finally, you want to show results only in the Engineering, Energy and Technology category.

6. **Click the Engineering, Energy and Technology check box in the Subject areas section**
   The check box you clicked is selected and the All subject areas check box is automatically deselected.

7. **Click Search**
   Web pages from scientific sources or about scientific topics that include your search phrase appear.

Finding a specialized search engine

Ask a reference librarian or instructor if they can recommend a specialized search engine for your research topic. Sometimes library Web pages that list resources in a subject area provide links to specialized search engines. Subject guides can also provide links.

FIGURE C-12: Scirus Advanced search page

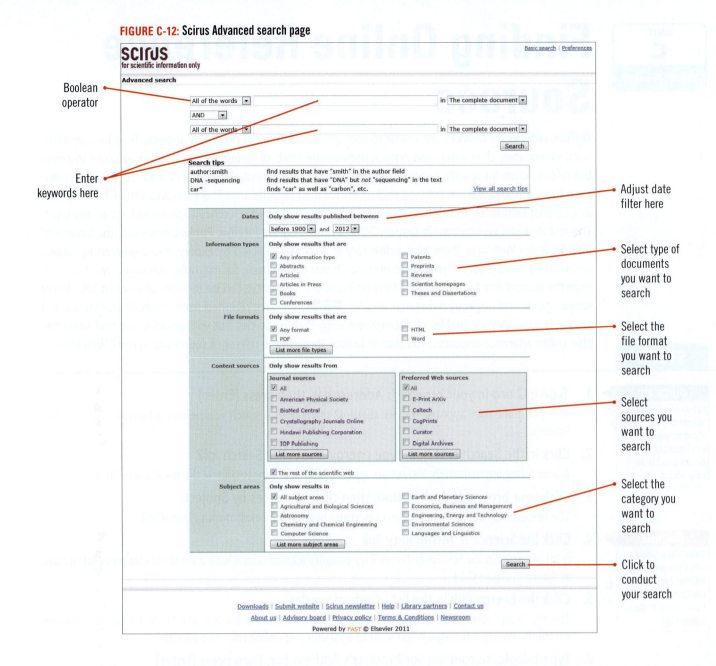

Internet Research

Finding Online Reference Sources

Online reference sources are similar to their print counterparts on library shelves. They include almanacs, dictionaries, directories, and encyclopedias—the kinds of resources you don't read cover to cover, but refer to often for specific information. Library Web sites almost always link to a variety of online reference sources, some of them licensed exclusively for their patrons' use. There are also virtual libraries, such as ipl2, that exist solely to bring together valuable Web sites and reference tools on just about any topic. The ipl2 Web site was created in January 2010 by merging the Internet Public Library and the Librarians' Internet Index Web sites. It contains a directory of Web sites selected by experts and organized by subject and then by subcategory. If your topic of research was the Internet, for example, you might want to reference the sources listed in Table C-5. Many online reference sources can be thought of as a combination of subject guide and a specialized search engine. You have returned from the EERE conference and are ready to finish your final list of alternative energy Web resources, but you would like to find a few reliable online reference resources. You decide to look through the reference sources at the ipl2 Web site.

STEPS

QUICK TIP

When you find good reference sites, add them to your browser's Favorites or Bookmarks file for easy access.

1. **Type ipl2.org in your browser's Address bar, then press [Enter]**
   The ipl2 home page appears. You see that ipl2 offers both a search engine and subject headings to drill through.

2. **Click in the Search text box, type energy, then click Search ipl2**
   A page listing approximately 500 results appears. Now you want to browse the resources by subject.

3. **Click your browser's Back button, then click Resources by Subject**
   The Resources by Subject main subject categories page appears as shown in Figure C-13.

TROUBLE

If nothing appears and if you are using Internet Explorer, click the Compatibility View button in the Address bar.

4. **Click the Science & Technology link**
   A list of results in the Science & Technology category appears, along with a list of subcategories on the left, as shown in Figure C-14.

5. **Click the Energy link in the list of subcategories**
   The results included in the Energy subcategory appear. Note on the left that there are no subcategories within the Energy subcategory. You want to try a different online reference source.

6. **Type infoplease.com in your browser's Address bar, then press [Enter]**
   The Infoplease home page appears.

7. **Click the Health & Science link in the list on the left**
   A list of subcategories in the Health & Science category appears.

8. **Click the Environment & Nature link to display its subcategories, then click the Energy link**
   The list of resources in the Energy subcategory appears.

TROUBLE

If you do not see this link, click the Renewable Energy Consumption in the U.S. by Source, 1989-2003 link. If you do not see the table, it might have opened in a new tab.

9. **Click the Renewable Energy Consumption in the U.S. by Source, 1989-2009 link**
   A table appears, showing how much renewable energy was used in the United States from 1989 to 2009.

FIGURE C-13: Subject headings on ipl2

Search text box

Links to categories

Links to subcategories that contain this result

FIGURE C-14: Results in the Science and Technology category with subcategories on ipl2

Category

Links to subcategories

Results in category

TABLE C-5: Resources for information on "the Internet" topic

name	URL	features
ipl2	ipl2.org	Provides reliable links to answer almost any Internet question; covers searching, Web design, history, law, children, and more
FILExt	filext.com	Lists most Internet file extensions; defines extensions and links to more information
Netiquette Home Page	albion.com/netiquette	Provides the basics of Netiquette, at work and at home; covers primarily online communication
Webopedia	webopedia.com	Covers computer and Internet terminology; provides paragraph encyclopedia definitions and links
Living Internet	livinginternet.com	Covers the Internet, the Web, email, chat, newsgroups, and mailing lists; articles include history and how-to information
Internet Tutorials	internettutorials.net	Covers using the Web, searching the Web, browsers, and training; provides links and how-to tips

Finding Specialty Information

Finding Government Information

Governments are prodigious producers and users of information. Large gateways, called **portals**, create access to different segments of government information, as shown in Table C-6. Portals originated in the commercial sector, with such sites as America Online and MSN that offered their version of "everything"—search engines, news, shopping, email, chat, and more. They each tried to create an attractive and useful site so that users would never go anywhere else to find information. The idea of a portal caught on, and now many other sites have carved out niches in various subject areas, especially in industry and government. These portals, which are limited by subject, are also referred to as **vortals**, or vertical portals. Portals and vortals are sometimes considered a type of specialized search engine. Government portals provide access to online information or to printed materials that you can purchase from government agencies or borrow from libraries. While attending the EERE conference in Washington, D.C., you heard of a good place to access government information online—USA.gov. You want to see what information you can find there about wind energy and other alternative energy resources.

STEPS

1. **Type usa.gov in your browser's Address bar, then press [Enter]**
   The USA.gov Web site opens. You can use either the Search text box or point to Explore Topics to display a list of topics you can use to drill down through subject headings.

2. **Click in the Search text box, type wind energy, then click SEARCH**
   A list of search results opens, as shown in Figure C-15. You want to expand your search to find results for alternative energy, renewable energy, or green energy. You can do this using the Advanced Search form.

3. **Click the Advanced Search link**

4. **Click in the All of these words text box, then delete your previous search query**

5. **Type energy in the All of these words text box**

6. **Click in the Any of these words text box, then type alternative renewable green**
   Compare your screen to Figure C-16.

7. **Click Search at the bottom of the page**
   The Web pages listed in the search results include the text *alternative energy, renewable energy,* or *green energy.*

TABLE C-6: Specialized government portals

name	URL	features
DirectGov	direct.gov.uk	Central and local government information for the United Kingdom
FedWorld	www.fedworld.gov	Sponsored by the National Technical Information Service (NTIS); includes scientific, technical, business, and engineering information; contains links to reports and publications available for purchase
Government of Canada	canada.gc.ca	Canadian federal, provincial, and municipal information
GPO Access	www.gpoaccess.gov	Contains links to federal publications; provides catalog of government documents available for purchase; contains a catalog of libraries that own specific documents
University of Michigan Government Documents Center	lib.umich.edu/ government- documents-center	Most complete guide to government information; contains links to local, state, national, and international government sites
USA.gov	usa.gov	Most comprehensive site for U.S. government information and services; contains links to over 20,000 federal and state government Web sites

FIGURE C-15: Search results for *wind energy* on USA.gov

Your search query

Search results

Advanced Search link

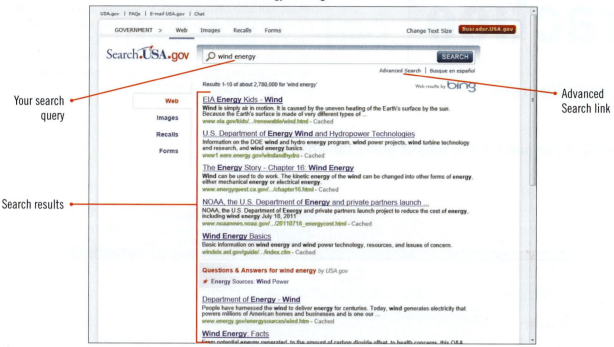

FIGURE C-16: Advanced Search page on USA.gov

Enter search query in these text boxes

Additional search options

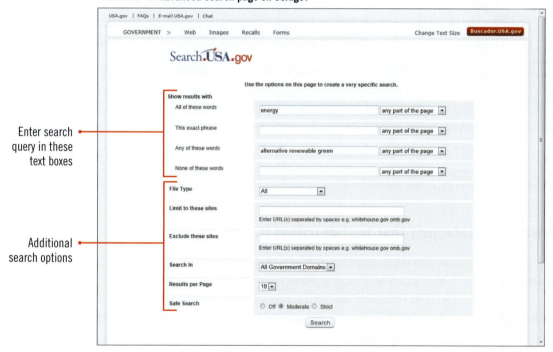

Finding state and provincial government sites

You might want to use government sites to locate Web sites for U.S. states or Canadian provinces. A search with *government* and the name of the state or province usually finds the official home page in the first few results. In addition, there are sites that contain pages that are portals to the official home pages of state and provincial government Web sites.

Practice

Concepts Review

For current SAM information, including versions and content details, visit SAM Central (http://www.cengage.com/samcentral). If you have a SAM user profile, you may have access to hands-on instruction, practice, and assessment of the skills covered in this unit. Since various versions of SAM are supported throughout the life of this text, check with your instructor for the correct instructions and URL/Web site for accessing assignments.

Label each of the parts in the subject guide shown in Figure C-17.

FIGURE C-17

Match each term with the statement that best describes it.

7. **Visible Web**

8. **Dynamically generated Web page**

9. **Specialized search engine**

10. **Drill down**

11. **ipl2**

12. **Portal**

13. **Online reference sources**

14. **Subject guide**

15. **Invisible Web**

a. Similar to print counterparts on library shelves

b. A gateway to large segments of related Web information

c. The portion of the Web accessible to traditional search engines and directories

d. Indexed Web pages maintained by experts and organized into hierarchical and alphabetical topics

e. A Web page that is generated when you request it

f. To browse or click through a hierarchy of topics and subtopics to reach links on a results page

g. An example of a virtual library

h. A search engine that limits the Web pages it searches by subject

i. The portion of the Web not accessible to traditional search engines

Select the best answer from the list of choices.

16. The invisible Web:
   a. is much smaller than the visible Web.
   b. consists mostly of dynamically generated Web pages.
   c. is also known as the deep Web.
   d. is not accessible.

17. Specialty sites might:
   a. give away some information but charge for some, too.
   b. require you to pay for the service.
   c. allow you a few free searches and ask you to pay for more.
   d. all of the above.

18. Which of the following are traits that all subject guides share?
   a. They are organized hierarchically and are selective in the Web sites they list.
   b. They are relatively small compared with search engines.
   c. They include annotations to the Web sites they index.
   d. All of the above.

19. A good place to search for information about businesses in the United Kingdom is:
   a. ipl2.
   b. Scoot.
   c. Switchboard.
   d. Yellowpages.ca.

20. A site with links to local, state, national, and international governments is:
   a. FirstGov.
   b. United States Government Printing Office.
   c. FedWorld.
   d. University of Michigan Documents Center.

21. One definition of browsing is:
   a. using a local search engine to search a subject guide.
   b. using criteria to evaluate a Web site.
   c. clicking through the hierarchy of topics at a subject guide.
   d. finding out who wrote a Web page.

22. A distributed subject guide:
   a. is maintained by one editor.
   b. is the same thing as a search engine.
   c. usually resides on one computer.
   d. might lack standardization.

23. Which of the following is *not* an example of an online reference source?
   a. Almanacs
   b. Encyclopedias
   c. Metasearch engine
   d. Dictionaries

Skills Review

1. **Understand subject guides.**

   If requested by your instructor, create a document listing the answers to the questions asked in the following exercises.

   a. Describe how subject guides are organized.

   b. Explain how subject guides limit the Web pages they index.

   c. Describe the two ways you can find a list of results in a subject guide.

   d. Explain why annotations help users determine which results are relevant.

   e. Explain why the results from a subject guide can be more useful than the results from a search engine.

2. **Use a subject guide.**

   a. Start your browser, then go to the Open Directory Project at **dmoz.org**.

   b. To find information about environmental health education, drill down to the results under the following path: Science/Environment/Environmental Health/Education. Note the path at the top of the page. If requested by your instructor, print or save this page of results.

   c. Return to the Open Directory Project home page, then display the subcategories in the Health category. Note the path at the top of the page.

   d. Display the subcategories in the Environmental Health subcategory. Note the path at the top of the page. Why do you think the path changed? If requested by your instructor, create a document listing the answer to this question.

   e. Display the results in the Education subcategory. Note the number of results after the path, and then examine the results and the annotations.

   f. Use the Search text box at the top of the page to conduct a search of the entire directory using the keywords *"environmental health" education*. Note the number of results. If requested by your instructor, print or save this page of results.

   g. Scroll down and examine the paths under each result. Are they the same or different as the drill-down path? If requested by your instructor, add the answer to this question to the document you created.

   h. Examine the list of results, identify the result that seems like it is the most relevant, and then follow that link to see if the Web page provides you with the information you want. If requested by your instructor, print or save this page.

3. **Understand the deep Web.**

   If requested by your instructor, create a document listing the answers to the questions asked in the following exercises.

   a. Explain what the invisible Web is.

   b. Explain what the visible Web is.

   c. Describe dynamically generated Web pages.

   d. Explain why results from specialty search engines and directories are higher-quality content than results from ordinary search engines.

4. **Search periodical databases.**

   a. Go to **magportal.com**.

   b. Drill down through the Education & Reference/Technology in Education categories. Click a subcategory that interests you. If requested by your instructor, print or save this page of results.

   c. Follow a link to one of the results. Read the article. (Note that you can click the "old articles" link to list articles that are older than a month or so.) If requested by your instructor, print or save this page.

   d. Click your browser's Back button, use the Search Articles text box to create a search query based on the article you just read, type the search query in the Search text box, and then conduct your search. If requested by your instructor, print or save this page of results.

   e. Examine your results, and then click a few links and scan the articles. Are they about the topic for which you searched? If not, rephrase your search query, and try your search again.

Skills Review (continued)

    f. Go to **nytimes.com**.

    g. Search for an article on this site using the same search query. If requested by your instructor, print or save this page of results.

    h. Examine the results. Are the stories about the right topic?

5. Find places.

    a. Go to **bing.com/maps**.

    b. Find the location of the Union Oyster House restaurant in Boston, Massachusetts.

    c. Zoom in until you can see the name of the street the restaurant is on. If requested by your instructor, print or save this page.

    d. Switch to Bird's eye view, and then zoom in until the image changes from a satellite image to a photo taken from the sky. (The details in the image will become clearer.)

    e. Switch to Aerial view.

    f. Switch to Streetside view by clicking the blue icon of a person.

    g. Go to **maps.google.com**, and then find the same restaurant. If requested by your instructor, print or save this page.

    h. Switch to Street view by dragging the orange icon of a person at the top of the Zoom bar to the location of the restaurant.

6. Find people and businesses.

    a. Go to **411locate.com**.

    b. Use the Locate a Person form to search for yours or a friend's information. If requested by your instructor, print or save this page of results.

    c. Click the View details link below yours or your friend's name on the results page. If there are no results, try a different name.

    d. Return to the home page on 411 Locate, and then use the Reverse Phone Lookup form to run a search on your home phone number. If requested by your instructor, print or save this page of results.

    e. Return to the Reverse Phone Lookup form on 411 Locate, and then use the Lookup form to search for your cell phone number. If requested by your instructor, print or save this page of results.

    f. Go to **switchboard.com**.

    g. Think of a business in your city or town, type its business category (such as accountants, newspapers, schools, or veterinarians) or business name, and type your city and state, and then click Search. (If there are no resulting businesses, go back and enter another type of business.) If requested by your instructor, print or save this page of results.

    h. Scroll down the results page. Is the business you thought of listed?

7. Use a specialized search engine.

    a. Go to **envirolink.org**. This is a specialized search engine for environmental Web sites.

    b. Use the Search text box to search for **green energy**. Note the number of results. If requested by your instructor, print or save this page of results.

    c. Return to the home page, and then view the subcategories in the Energy category. Note the number of results in each of the following subcategories (as indicated by the number in parentheses after the subcategory name): Biomass, Geothermal Energy, Solar Energy, and Wind Energy. If requested by your instructor, print or save this page of results.

    d. Examine the results in the Wind Energy subcategory. If requested by your instructor, print or save this page of results.

    e. Click one of the results to examine the information presented on that site.

Skills Review (continued)

8. **Find online reference sources.**
   a. Go to **ipl2.org**.
   b. Click Special Collections Created by ipl2, and then click the A+ Research/Writing Guide button. If requested by your instructor, print or save this page.
   c. Click the Table of Contents link, and then explore the resource.
   d. Return to the ipl2 home page, click Resources by Subject, click the Reference link, and then click the Style and Writing Guides subcategory link. If requested by your instructor, print or save this page of results.
   e. Scroll down and click the Purdue University Online Writing Lab (OWL) link. Click the link on the OWL site that leads you to information on the APA style. Read this information. If requested by your instructor, print or save this page.
   f. Return to the Purdue University Online Writing Lab (OWL) home page, and then click the link that leads you to information on the MLA style. Read this information. If requested by your instructor, print or save this page.

9. **Find government information.**
   a. Go to **usa.gov**.
   b. Conduct a search using the search query **senator**. Examine the wide range of results. If requested by your instructor, print or save this page of results.
   c. Click the Advanced Search link.
   d. Make sure *senator* is in the All of these words text box.
   e. Click in the This exact phrase text box, and then type **committee chair**.
   f. Click Search at the bottom of the page. How did this narrow the search results? If requested by your instructor, print or save this page of results.

Independent Challenge 1

You want to start exporting the products your business sells to Canada and Australia. You want to do some research to find information on each country's regulations.

a. Go to the Web site for the Canadian government at **canada.gc.ca**.
b. Conduct a search using the search query **importing goods**. Examine the results. If requested by your instructor, print or save this page of results.
c. On the right, under Narrow by Department, click the Foreign Affairs and International Trade link. If requested by your instructor, print or save this page of results. Examine the results again, click one that seems the most likely to contain the answers to your questions, and read the page that opens.
d. Go to the Web site for the Australian government at **australia.gov.au**.
e. Conduct a search on this site using the same search query as in step b above. If requested by your instructor, print or save this page of results.
f. Examine the results, click one that seems the most likely to contain the answers to your questions, and read the page that opens.

Independent Challenge 2

You are with a firm that specializes in designing Web sites for banks. Your company is going to design the Web site for the National Irish Bank, and you need to fly to Dublin to visit several banks. You need to look up locations of this and other banks in the greater Dublin area.

a. Go to **goldenpages.ie**, a yellow pages site listing businesses in Ireland.
b. Create a search query to find the National Irish Bank in the city of Dublin. If requested by your instructor, print or save this page of results.

Independent Challenge 2 (continued)

c. Use the map and the list of results to find 10 other banks in the city of Dublin somewhat near the National Irish Bank. If requested by your instructor, print or save this page.

Advanced Challenge Exercise

- Use the Goldenpages.ie site to find companies located in the city of Dublin that design Web sites. If requested by your instructor, print or save this page of results.
- Explore the descriptions for several of the Web site design businesses, and examine their Web sites.
- Choose one result, and then use the More link to find the URL of the company's Web site. If requested by your instructor, print or save this page.

Independent Challenge 3

You and a business associate are driving in Great Britain from London to Manchester to visit some clients. As you haven't driven there before, you want to get driving directions.

a. Go to the British MapQuest Web site at **mapquest.co.uk**.

b. Find the section for directions.

c. Enter the appropriate to and from locations and get the directions. (Note that because the Web site identifies the location of your computer, you might need to type **England** after each city name.)

d. On the resulting directions page, locate the Print link, and then click the link.

e. Type your name in the Notes section, deselect the Map check box, select the Without Advertisement check box, and then print the directions.

Advanced Challenge Exercise

- Go to the North American MapQuest Web site at **mapquest.com**.
- Click the link to get driving directions. Find the driving distance between Quebec, QC, and Vancouver, BC. Note the total distance. If requested by your instructor, print or save this page.
- Select the option to calculate the directions so that the driving occurs all within Canada and not within the United States. Is the total driving distance longer or shorter than your first search? If requested by your instructor, print or save this page.

Real Life Independent Challenge

The first step in getting a job interview in today's highly competitive job market is to create a top-notch résumé. Subject guides can provide invaluable resources to help you prepare the best possible résumé. Because ipl2 is one of the most comprehensive hand-crafted subject guides on the Web, you decide to check it for help with your résumé.

a. Go to **ipl2.org**.

b. Display the list of categories, and then drill down to find the Employment subcategory in the Business and Economics category. If requested by your instructor, print or save this page of results.

c. Click one of the resources listed that offers advice or samples of résumé and cover letters. Explore the suggestions and examples of how to prepare a résumé.

d. Return to the ipl2 home page, and use the Search text box to find results for the search query **resume**. Examine the results. If requested by your instructor, print or save this page of results.

Visual Workshop

Find the Web page shown in Figure C-18. To start, go the home page of the Open Directory project (**dmoz.org**). After you find the page, click one of the results.

FIGURE C-18

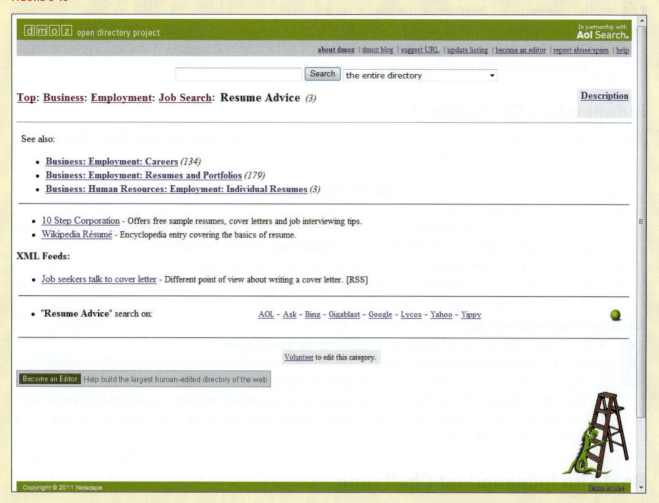

Searching the Social Web

As explained in Unit A, **social media platforms** include social networks, blogs, microblogs, video and photo sharing sites, social news sites and article directories, and Q&A (Question-and-Answer) sites, as well as bookmarking sites and news aggregators. People use social media platforms to create and maintain relationships. There are hundreds of millions of social media participants who collaborate to produce an almost endless stream of content that is posted, discussed, reviewed, voted on, and frequently "tagged" with keywords for classification and location purposes. This massive and highly varied social content is hosted on hundreds of thousands of individual **social media sites**, which are collectively referred to as the **Social Web**. Searching the Social Web is the process of locating a wide variety of content on social media platforms. Understanding the distinctive search capabilities, features, and limitations of each type of social media platform is the key to efficiently and effectively locating the content you want on the Social Web.  At a conference in Washington, D.C., on renewable energy, you met several experts in windmill turbines and biomass as a renewable energy. Bob Johnson, the reference librarian, suggests that you use the Social Web to discover additional experts and information on the subject.

OBJECTIVES

Identify social media platforms

Understand social media searches

Search social networks

Navigate the blogosphere

Scan microblogs

Search video and photo sharing sites

Search social news sites and article directories

Find answers with Q&A sites

Use social media search engines

Identifying Social Media Platforms

A wide variety of social media platforms exist on the Social Web, and each type provides a different way for participants to connect with each other. Table D-1 lists popular social media sites and ranks them in order of number of visitors per month. These rankings will change frequently, as people's tastes evolve and new offerings become available.  Before you begin searching the Social Web to find new sources of information on alternative energy, you decide to explore the types of social media platforms.

DETAILS

The following are common categories of social media platforms:

QUICK TIP
You can search social networks like LinkedIn to find people you know who are currently employed by companies you want to work for.

- **Social networks**

  Social networks are online communities where people form relationships based on everything from friendship and workplace affiliations to common interests and shared beliefs. To facilitate this, these sites typically encourage users to create profiles about themselves. Popular social networks include Facebook, MySpace, and LinkedIn. Some pundits predict Google+ will join these ranks.

- **Blogs**

  A **blog** (short for We**b log**) is regularly published content, such as commentaries, opinions, and announcements, in the form of text, images, and video. Most blogs are interactive, encouraging readers to publish comments, which bloggers often respond to. When a blog owner publishes an entry or a reader publishes a comment, it is referred to as **posting**. The term **post** also refers to a published blog entry.

- **Microblogs**

  A **microblog** is a blog that significantly limits the length of posts. Most microblog posts consist of short sentences and links. Twitter, with over 200 million users, is the leading microblogging site. Twitter limits "tweets" to 140 characters. It is common for "Twitterers" to include a link to a site with more detailed information.

- **Video and photo sharing sites**

  People upload and share video clips and images using **video** and **photo sharing sites**. Typically, videos and photos can be shared with the public or restricted for private viewings. YouTube is far and away the most visited video sharing site.

- **Social news sites and article directories**

  Social news sites enable users to submit news stories or other Web pages and vote on news stories posted by others. The most popular content appears on the coveted front pages of these sites. **Article directories** provide content that typically must be approved to be published. EzineArticles, whose home page is shown in Figure D-1, is one of the most popular article directories among readers, Internet marketers, and search engines, with a respectively high Google page rank of 6.

- **Social bookmarking sites and news aggregators**

  A **social bookmarking site**, such as Delicious, MyLinkvault, or BlinkList, lets people store and describe their favorite Web pages with tags, allowing other users to search for popular content. A **news aggregator**, such as Google News, is a Web site that collects headlines from news sources and lists them as links.

- **Q&A sites and Wiki sites**

  Q&A (**Question and Answer**) **sites** allow people to pose a question and receive answers back from anyone willing and (it is hoped) knowledgeable enough to reply. Quora (founded by two former top Facebook executives) is an up and coming Q&A site on which over 400,000 users registered during its first year. A **wiki** is server software that lets anyone create and modify Web page content. A wiki (Hawaiian for *quick*) makes it easy to build and interlink Web pages, encouraging group participation in building Web content.

FIGURE D-1: Home page on EzineArticles.com

Current number of authors

Categories of articles available

Click to join the site as an author

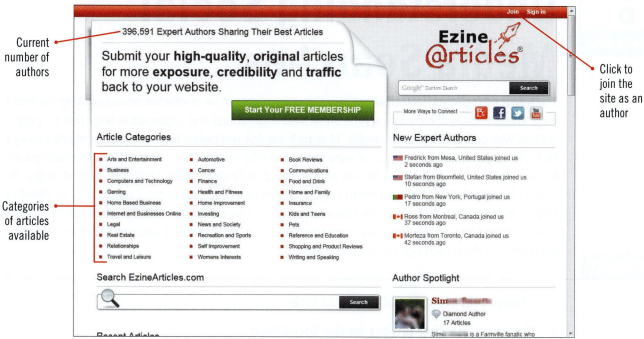

TABLE D-1: Popular social media sites

social media site	type	monthly visitors* (millions)	social media site	type	monthly visitors* (millions)
Facebook facebook.com	Social network	700	**Photobucket** photobucket.com	Photo sharing site	75.5
YouTube youtube.com	Video sharing site	450	**Blogger** www.blogger.com	Blog hosting site	75
Wikipedia wikipedia.org	Wiki	250	**Ning** ning.com	Social network	60
Twitter twitter.com	Microblogging site	200	**Tumblr** tumblr.com	Blog hosting site	60
WordPress wordpress.com	Blog hosting site	150	**eHow** ehow.com	Article directory	55
LinkedIn linkedin.com	Social network	100	**Digg** digg.com	Social news site	25.1
Flickr flickr.com	Photo sharing site	90	**Orkut** orkut.com	Social network	15.5
MySpace myspace.com	Social network	80.5	**Hi5** hi5.com	Social network	11.5

*Estimated unique monthly visitors according to eBiz|MBA Knowledgebase, July 2011.

Internet Research

Understanding Social Media Searches

The search strategies you learned about in earlier units might not be as effective when searching the Social Web. This is because the content on the Social Web is generated and organized in large part by people without Web design skills, so the benefits of **search engine optimization**—the process of fine-tuning a Web site so that it ranks at the top of search engine results—are not as prevalent. To further complicate matters, each social media platform has its own set of distinctive search tools and methodologies. To search effectively for specific social media content hosted on a multitude of social media sites, you need to employ unique search strategies to find the information you are looking for.  You realize that to find specific information on the Social Web you need to understand the search tools and methodologies for effectively searching each type of social media platform.

DETAILS

To enhance your searching of the Social Web:

- **Become a member of sites on the Social Web**

  Being a member of specific sites on the Social Web allows you to use the site's resources more completely. For example, as a member of a social news site, you can add your vote to an article's rating. Also, although many social networks allow you to search for members without actually being a member yourself, the publicly available information is often limited to nonmembers. On some sites, such as Facebook, members can limit the details that people who are not listed as a "friend" of the member can see.

- **Understand tags**

  Tags are key words that identify the contents of blog and microblog posts, videos, photos, articles, and questions on Q&A sites. By tagging content, the content owners are giving search engines another key word to index. Sites that allow users to tag content also allow you to search for content using tags or, sometimes, to simply click a tag in a list or in a tag cloud, to display content tagged with the word you clicked. A **tag cloud** is a presentation of tags in which the font size of the text indicates how often the tag is used. Figure D-2 shows a tag cloud generated from the text in this unit on TagCrowd.com.

QUICK TIP

You can use password managers, such as RoboForm, to automatically log into multiple social media sites with a click of a button.

- **Learn about social media search engines**

  Social media search engines search multiple social media sites simultaneously, typically in real time. For example, you can find the newest content on social networks, discover recent posts on blogs, track conversations as they take place among experts on microblogs such as Twitter, and see the latest social news, all at the same time. However, your searches are limited to what is publically available, unless you are logged into the social media sites that require registration.

- **Use blog search engines**

  Blog search engines index only blogs so when you use them, you don't have to filter through results from other types of Web pages. You can usually specify whether you want to search for key words in blog titles, the posts themselves, or tags assigned to blogs.

- **Use search engines built into sites on the Social Web**

  Most sites on the Social Web include built-in search engines that you can use to search for content on that site. Usually, the sites also provide an Advanced Search page and allow you to use Boolean operators to narrow your search and help you find the exact content you are searching for.

answers article blog blogosphere content create decide directories

energy engines facebook information limited linkedin media

member microblog networks news operator page people photo

platforms popular posts published question ranks reference renewable

search sharing sites social specific suggests tag

topic tweet twitter users video web

More popular tag   Less popular tag

Recognize the wisdom of the crowd

Social media taps into the power of mass collaboration of community participation and group contributions to produce what has commonly been called the "wisdom of the crowd." In contrast to relying on a single expert to render an informed opinion, the wisdom of crowds in social media draw on the collective opinions to build a broad and extensive consensus. Wikipedia, a collaboratively built online encyclopedia, is a prime example of this. A wide variety of experts worked together to create an extensive and reliable online knowledge base. When inaccurate information does appear in Wikipedia, it is corrected by an "army" of experts (Wikipedians) who watch and maintain the material in this online encyclopedia. (Indeed, several studies have shown that the information in Wikipedia is more accurate than the content in a traditional encyclopedia.)

Internet Research

Searching Social Networks

Social networks, such as Facebook and LinkedIn, enable people to easily establish relationships and virtual communities by sharing personal profiles, participating in groups, and exchanging private and public messages. Facebook is a social network that originally was intended to be used by college students, but has grown to be the top-ranked social network with participants from a wide range of ages and walks of life. LinkedIn is a social network that targets professionals and business people, making it a great resource for locating expertise in a variety of fields. Because LinkedIn has a highly structured format, you can find people and businesses with simple keyword searches. For example, if you want to find only people currently working for a particular company, you can enter the name of the company and specify that they are current employees of the organization. Although you can search or browse for a person on LinkedIn or Facebook without being a member, the profiles available to nonmembers searching the sites are typically quite limited (for example, they often lack contact information and any depth about the person's background). And on Facebook, members must "friend" you—identify you as someone who can see their full profiles. 🎨 During the renewable energy conference in Washington, D.C., you learned that the largest manufacturer of electric wind turbines in the U.S. is a company called GE Wind Energy. You decide to use LinkedIn to find employees of this company with expertise in this technology.

STEPS

1. **Start your browser, type linkedin.com in the Address bar, then press [Enter]**

   The home page for the social network LinkedIn appears in your browser. Although you can search for members on LinkedIn, to take advantage of its full search capabilities and gain access to the details of the current members, you need to be a member yourself.

2. **If you are a LinkedIn member, click the Sign in link, then, in the appropriate text boxes, type your email address and your password to log in; if you are not a LinkedIn member, enter your first and last names, email address, and a password, click Join Today, then follow the instructions to fill in the necessary information to create a profile**

   After you log into LinkedIn, you will see your home page. There is a menu bar across the top.

3. **Click Profile in the menu bar, then click View Profile**

   A page similar to the one shown in Figure D-3 appears. Each member of LinkedIn provides information about his or her work experience and other relevant information to be displayed on the Profile page. You can search the LinkedIn network using the Search text box at the right end of the menu bar.

4. **Click the People button on the right end of the menu bar**

   A menu opens listing additional categories you can search, including Jobs, Companies, Answers, Inbox, and Groups. To take advantage of the LinkedIn search capabilities, you will switch to the Advanced search form.

5. **Click Advanced to the right of the Search text box**

   The LinkedIn Advanced People Search page appears, as shown in Figure D-4. You want to search for people who currently are employed by GE Wind Energy.

6. **Click in the Company text box, type GE Wind Energy, click the Current or past list arrow beneath the Company text box, click Current, then click the Search button**

   A list of job titles and locations of people that currently work for GE Wind Energy appears sorted by relevance to the search query, as shown in Figure D-5.

7. **Click several of the links in the search results, and examine their profiles to find someone with expertise in wind turbines**

   Many of the profiles withhold the member's name to prevent unwanted contact from job recruiters trolling LinkedIn looking for people to fill positions. If this were a real-world situation, you would need to email the person to make direct contact. LinkedIn offers more access to other members' details for a fee.

FIGURE D-3: Home page of a LinkedIn member

Click options in the menu bar to edit your profile, manage your contacts and groups, and other settings

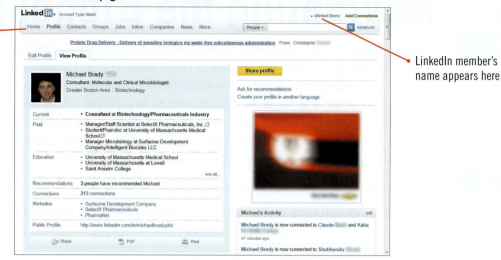

LinkedIn member's name appears here

FIGURE D-4: LinkedIn's Advanced People Search page

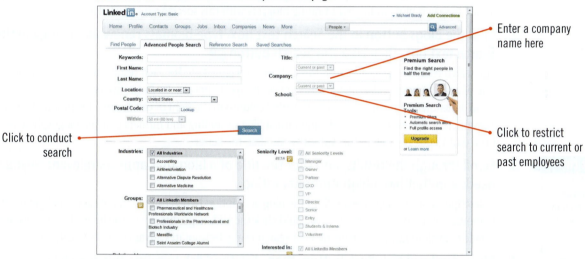

Enter a company name here

Click to conduct search

Click to restrict search to current or past employees

FIGURE D-5: Search results for current employees of GE Wind Energy on LinkedIn

Click to sort results based on other criteria

Click to expand results to include more information about each member

Finding discussion groups or forums

A **discussion board** provides the means for people to conduct conversations online by exchanging messages asynchronously. Topics are typically organized into **discussion groups** (also called **discussion forums**). Within a discussion group, topics are further broken into subtopics called **threads** which arrange messages hierarchically, using indentation to reveal the chronological flow of the conversations. You can find discussion groups dedicated to specific topics by using discussion group search engines, such as Google Groups, Yahoo Groups, Boardreader, and BoardTracker. Social networks also often have active discussion groups, but you need to join the social network to search for and join these groups.

Navigating the Blogosphere

The **blogosphere** is made up of all blogs and their interconnections. The blogosphere continues to grow, in large part due to sites that allow people to create blogs for free, such as Google's Blogger, which has over 70 million estimated unique monthly visitors. You can search for information on individual blog sites, but, fortunately, blog search engines have evolved to help people quickly and efficiently locate specific information in the blogosphere. Table D-2 describes some of the popular blog search engines. To help you find more information and experts about biomass as a renewable energy, Bob suggests you search the blogosphere to find other informed opinions on this subject.

STEPS

1. **Type technorati.com in your browser's Address bar, then press [Enter]**
   The Technorati home page appears. Note that the top of the page contains a variety of categories you can click to view popular blogs in each category. The page also includes a Search text box, and to the left of the Search text box are the Blogs and Posts buttons. These buttons allow you to specify whether you want the search to return blog titles or posts. Since you want to find experts in biomass as a renewable energy, you decide to search blogs in hopes of finding bloggers with this specialized knowledge.

2. **Click the Blogs button in the Search text box, type biomass renewable energy in the Search text box, then click the Search button** 🔍
   The search results appear, similar to those shown in Figure D-6. For each result, the blog title, blog URL, the title of a recent post, and a brief description of that post appears. An Authority rating is also given for each result as denoted by the number in the "Auth:" column to the right of each result. Technorati Authority uses a proprietary algorithm to evaluate and rank a blog's standing and influence in the blogosphere on a scale from 0 to 1,000. The higher the Authority number, the better.

QUICK TIP
You can click the page numbers at the top and bottom of the search results to see additional search returns.

3. **Scroll through the results, and click the title of a blog that appears relevant to your needs and that has a high Authority rating**
   A description of the blog appears. Scan the blog description to determine if it appears to belong to an expert in biomass as a renewable energy. You could click the URL to go directly to the blog. However, for now, you decide to explore further by refining your search using Technorati's advanced search features.

4. **Click your browser's Back button, then click the Click to refine this search link**
   The Refine options page appears. Here you can choose to change whether blog titles or posts are returned. You can also choose whether to search in blogs, on news sites, or both (the "all" option). In addition, you can restrict your search by topic and Authority rating. Finally, you can order search results by relevance (the default) or date. To narrow your search to experts dedicated to "green" energy sources, you decide to refine your search by category.

5. **Click the Filter by list arrow, click Green, then click the Refine this search button**
   The search results are refreshed, showing just the blogs in the green category. Notice that you have significantly reduced the number of blogs to examine.

6. **Click a blog title that appears relevant to your needs and that has a high Authority rating, read the blog description, then click the blog's URL to navigate to the blog's site**
   The blog appears in your browser window with the most recent post at the top. To confirm the Authority rating for yourself, you want to find out about the blogger's credentials. Most bloggers post information about themselves on an About Me page.

7. **Click the About Me link (or something similar), then read the blog author's description of him or herself**
   Finally, you should read a few blog posts so you can determine if the blog content suits your needs.

8. **Read the first few posts in the blog**

FIGURE D-6: Search results for *biomass renewable energy* on Technorati

Click to restrict the search to blogs

Click to view blogs by category

Click to search content based on tags

Blog title, blog URL, and title of recent post

Click to restrict the search to posts

Search text box

Authority rating

TABLE D-2: Blog search engines

blog search engine	URL	search features
Google Blog Search	blogsearch.google.com	• Search by exact phrase for posts • Search by title or author • Search by blog or post dates
Technorati	technorati.com	• Search for posts or blog titles • Browse the blog directory • Search by tags • Filter results by Authority rating • Sort results by relevance or date
BlogPulse	blogpulse.com	• Sort results by date or by relevance • Search using advanced criteria
Icerocket	icerocket.com	• Search by exact phrase for posts • Restrict search to specific domains • Restrict search to a specific author and date range

Understanding RSS

RSS (Real Simple Syndication) is a protocol that gives you the ability to selectively subscribe to automatic updates from a wide variety of social media platforms. The updated content is often called a feed or channel. Most social media sites offer an RSS feed to their sites, as denoted by the 🔲 icon. An **RSS reader** lets you receive and view RSS feeds, typically showing the titles and brief descriptions of fresh content, making it simple to skim the list and then find and click a relevant item, displaying the entire article, post, or video. It is unlikely that the current vibrant and growing Social Web would exist without RSS. Without RSS (or a similar service), it would be necessary to manually visit each of these sites to discover and read new content, thus vastly restricting the scope and magnitude of the Social Web. Popular RSS readers include Google Reader, RSSOwl, Sage, as well as built-in RSS readers in products like Microsoft Internet Explorer and Outlook.

Scanning Microblogs

Although there are other microblog sites, such as FriendFeed, Tumblr, Jaiku, and Plurk, Twitter's huge following and rich search capabilities make it the microblog of choice for research. Figure D-7 shows the Twitter home page, and Figure D-8 shows one Twitter author's home page. Searches are conducted on Twitter more than a billion times a day. Twitter authors, or twitterers, make liberal use of tags to make it easier to locate a tweet about a particular topic. In addition, a tweet author can tag a tweet by using **hashtags**, which are words in a tweet that the author identifies by typing the pound, or hash, sign operator (#) before the word to create topical categories that others can search for. You can find tweets tagged with a specific hashtag by placing the hash sign operator in front of a word in the Search text box. Another powerful Twitter operator is the at sign (@). To use this operator, type the @ symbol in front a twitterer's name to return all messages that contain that name. And you can use the near: operator to find search terms tweeted by people near a specific location. (To find a complete list of Twitter search operators, go to search.twitter.com/operators.) 🎨 At the renewable energy conference in Washington, D.C., you attended a panel discussion about geothermal energy. You decide to search for discussions about this topic using Twitter.

STEPS

1. **Type twitter.com in your browser's Address bar, then press [Enter]**

   The Twitter home page appears. See Figure D-7.

2. **Click in the Search Twitter text box, type geothermal energy, then click the Search button** 🔍

   A page listing the top (most popular) tweets containing *geothermal energy* appears. Each result begins with the name of the twitterer, followed by the beginning of the tweet, and ending with the information on when the tweet was posted. In each message text, the key words from your search are in bold. You can expand the search to include all tweets, not only the top tweets.

3. **Click the Top arrow above the list of results, then click All**

   A new search results page appears listing all the results, not just the top ones. You decide to use the hashtag search operator to search for tweets tagged with the hashtag *geothermal*.

4. **Delete the text in the Search text box, type #geothermal in the Search text box, then click** 🔍

   This search returns a list of all the tweets with the hashtag *geothermal*. The main drawback to searching using a hashtag is that tweeters do not use hashtag operators consistently, so it requires a trial-and-error approach to find a hashtag that returns the results you want. You have heard that the twitterer whose user name is deepgreendesign posts interesting tweets, so you decide to use the @ search operator to find tweets that mention this user name.

5. **Replace the text in the Search text box with @deepgreendesign, then click** 🔍

   A list of all the messages that mention that user's name appears. When you search for tweets that mention a user name, you might see results that contain tweets that resemble a conversation; for example, a tweet posted in reply to a tweet by deepgreendesign might say "Thanks for that info." Finally, you decide to find tweets that mention the search phrase *geothermal energy* made by people who are located near Portland, Oregon.

6. **Replace the text in the Search text box with geothermal energy near:"Portland, OR", then click** 🔍

   Tweets posted by people near Portland, Oregon, are displayed. Naturally, the length of this list will vary, depending upon the activity level. It can even be empty on holidays or other special occasions.

FIGURE D-7: Twitter home page

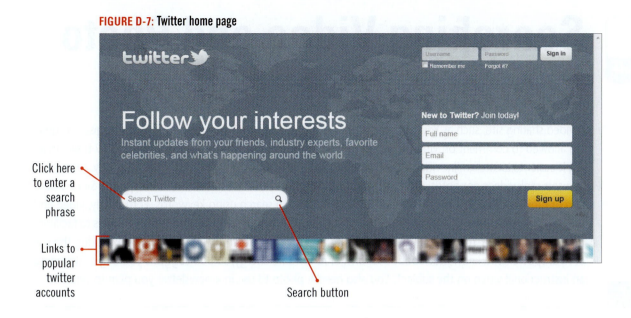

Click here to enter a search phrase

Links to popular twitter accounts

Search button

FIGURE D-8: An author's home page on Twitter

Post directed to this user

Post containing a hashtag

Searching Video and Photo Sharing Sites

A video sharing site, such as YouTube, lets users upload videos for public viewing. Typically, registered users are allowed to comment on videos and tag them with descriptive keywords to group them by topic, making it easier to locate similar videos. Photo sharing sites, such as Flickr, work much the same way. Many sites let users rank videos or photos, with the most popular ones featured on the sites' home pages. Since videos and graphics are not text based, they are inherently hard to search using keywords. Fortunately, video and photo sharing sites (along with other third parties) have developed sophisticated search engines to facilitate this process. 🎨 You heard at the conference that several cities in the Northwest are exploring the use of hydropower. You know little about this form of renewable energy, so Bob suggests you begin by finding an instructional video on the subject. You also need a photo to use in a newsletter you plan to send.

STEPS

1. **Type youtube.com in your browser's Address bar, then press [Enter]**
   The YouTube home page appears with the Search text box at the top.

QUICK TIP
You can narrow video search returns to just the clips that have your keywords in their titles with the intitle: operator (for example, intitle:hydroelectric).

2. **Click in the Search text box, type how hydropower works, then click the Search button**
   A list of results appears. Identifying information about each video appears to the right of each thumbnail of a frame from each video, as shown in Figure D-9, including a link to the creator's YouTube **channel**, which is the home page of the account holder listing all the video clips uploaded by this person.

3. **Scroll through the results, then click the thumbnail or the title of one you want to view**
   When the video begins playing, thumbnails of related videos appear on the right; upon completion of the video, other related videos are displayed in the Play window. When you conduct a search on YouTube, the results are sorted by relevance, but you can change it so they are sorted by upload date, view count, or rating.

4. **Click the Back button in your browser, click the Relevance button next to Sort by on the right side of the window, then click View count on the menu**
   The results are sorted from the most watched to the least. The Filter button on the left lets you filter results based on upload times, categories, duration, and features. Next, you need a photo for a newsletter.

5. **Type flickr.com in your browser's Address bar, then press [Enter]**
   The home page for Flickr appears. Flickr provides many advanced search features. To view its Search page, simply click the Search link to the right of the empty Search text box at the top of the page.

QUICK TIP
Alternative ways to search Flickr are TagGalaxy, FlickrStorm on Zoo-m.com, LiteFlick, and FlickrBabel.

6. **Click the Search link to the right of the Search text box**
   The Search page appears with tabs to search for photos, groups, or people (the photographers) on the site. You can also choose to search the descriptions of the videos or only the tags assigned by the photographer. To conduct an even more sophisticated search, you can use the Advanced Search page.

7. **Click the Advanced Search link to display the Advanced Search page, click in the Search for text box, type hydroelectric generator, then click the Screenshots / Screencasts and Illustration/Art / Animation/CGI check boxes**
   By default, the option of searching the full text of the photo descriptions is selected, as is the Photos / Videos check box in the Search by content type section and the Photos & Videos option in the Search by media type section. Compare your screen to Figure D-10.

QUICK TIP
You can right-click a picture to select different sizes to display.

8. **Scroll to the bottom of the page, then click the Search button**
   A list of image search results appears. You can click a result to display a larger version of the photo with the name of the creator of the image in the upper-right corner of the page. If you click the name, that photographer's or organization's **photostream**—the home page of the account holder—appears.

Approximate number of search results

Click to filter the search results

Thumbnail of a frame from the video

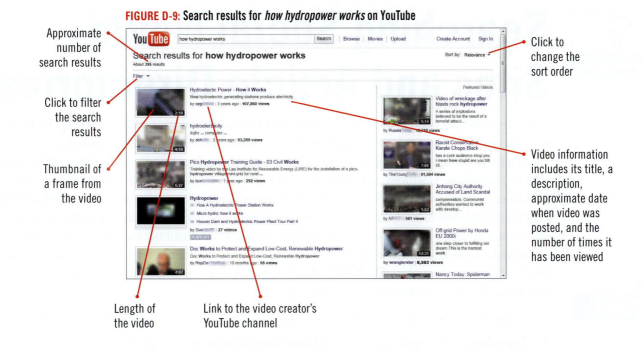

Click to change the sort order

Video information includes its title, a description, approximate date when video was posted, and the number of times it has been viewed

Length of the video

Link to the video creator's YouTube channel

Search expression

Click to search for all of the words (AND), any of the words (OR), or the exact phrase

Use to filter search results by dates you specify

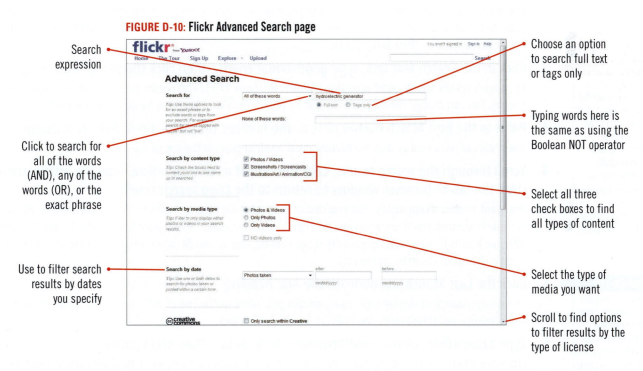

Choose an option to search full text or tags only

Typing words here is the same as using the Boolean NOT operator

Select all three check boxes to find all types of content

Select the type of media you want

Scroll to find options to filter results by the type of license

Understanding copyrights and licenses

Almost every image on a photo or video sharing site is protected by copyright. Many images on Flickr.com are made available through a Creative Commons license, which allows content owners to describe the rights they retain while allowing them to share their content. There are several types of Creative Commons licenses, as described on their Web site (creativecommons.org/ licenses/) and on Flickr (flickr.com/ creativecommons/). To check the copyright restrictions for a particular photo on Flickr, display the photo's page, then click the link under License. This reveals the type of license assigned to the image. Photos that are not licensed under Creative Commons licenses will have "All rights reserved," "Request to license link," or something similar under the License heading. If you want to restrict your search to photos that have a Creative Commons license, on the Advanced Search page click the appropriate check box in the search form.

Internet Research

Searching Social News Sites and Article Directories

Social news sites are good places to find links to popular news articles that other users liked. Highly frequented social news sites include Digg, Reddit, and StumbleUpon. Article directories are a good source for locating original articles that have not been published elsewhere. Popular article directories include Knol, eHow, EzineArticles, GoArticles, and ArticlesBase. To optimize for search engine indexing, most article directories tend to have articles that run 400 to 500 words in length. They also have a **keyword density** of approximately two to three percent, which means that two to three percent of the words in each article are words that people would tend to use to search for information about the topic in the article. You can find popular news stories and well-written, popular articles about specific topics quickly if you use the search engines on these sites. With Bob's urging, you decide to use social news sites and article directories to learn more about geothermal energy.

STEPS

1. **Type digg.com in your browser's Address bar, then press [Enter]**

   The home page for Digg appears. The most popular news stories as voted by users are displayed on the home page. Note that some social news sites use human editors or a combination of votes and editors to select the stories that appear on their home pages.

   TROUBLE

   If results do not appear, click after the text in the Search text box, and then press [Enter]. If it still doesn't work, click the Compatibility View button in the Address bar if you are using Internet Explorer, then try the [Enter] method again.

2. **Click in the Search text box, type geothermal energy, then click the Search button** 🔍

   The search results appear, similar to those shown in Figure D-11. The results are sorted by relevance (Best Match). You can change the sort order to sort by popularity (Most Dugg) or by date (Most Recent).

3. **Point to the Best Match button next to the number of results, then click Most Dugg**

   The results are re-sorted so that the highest rated result appears at the top of the list.

4. **Scroll through the search results, click the title of a relevant article, scan the article, then close the tab or browser window to return to the Digg search results**

   You want to find recent articles, so you decide to restrict the search results to those published in the last month. To do this, you'll use a link on the right side of the search results page to filter the results. You can filter the results by date (Age), popularity (Digg Count), type of media (news, images, or videos), and topics (such as Business, Lifestyle, and so on).

   QUICK TIP

   The news aggregator popUrls collects headlines (in near real time) from top social news sites and gathers them in one place for convenience.

5. **Click the Last Month link beneath the Age heading**

   The results change to display only those articles published in the last month. Impressed with articles you found using a social news site, you next try an article directory.

6. **Type ezinearticles.com in your browser's Address bar, then press [Enter]**

   The EzineArticles home page appears. Recently approved articles appear below the list of article categories. Since EzineArticles relies on the Google search engine, you can use all the Google operators to search EzineArticles for content. You want to find all the articles at EzineArticles with *geothermal energy* in their titles, so you decide to use Google's intitle: advanced search operator.

7. **Click in the Search text box, type intitle:"geothermal energy", then click the Search button**

   EzineArticles displays your Google search of its article database, with only the articles that have *geothermal energy* in their titles, similar to Figure D-12.

8. **Scroll through the search results, then click the title of a relevant article**

   The article appears in EzineArticles. After reading the article, you come to the conclusion that both social news sites and article directories are a powerful way to find information.

FIGURE D-11: Search results for *geothermal energy* on Digg

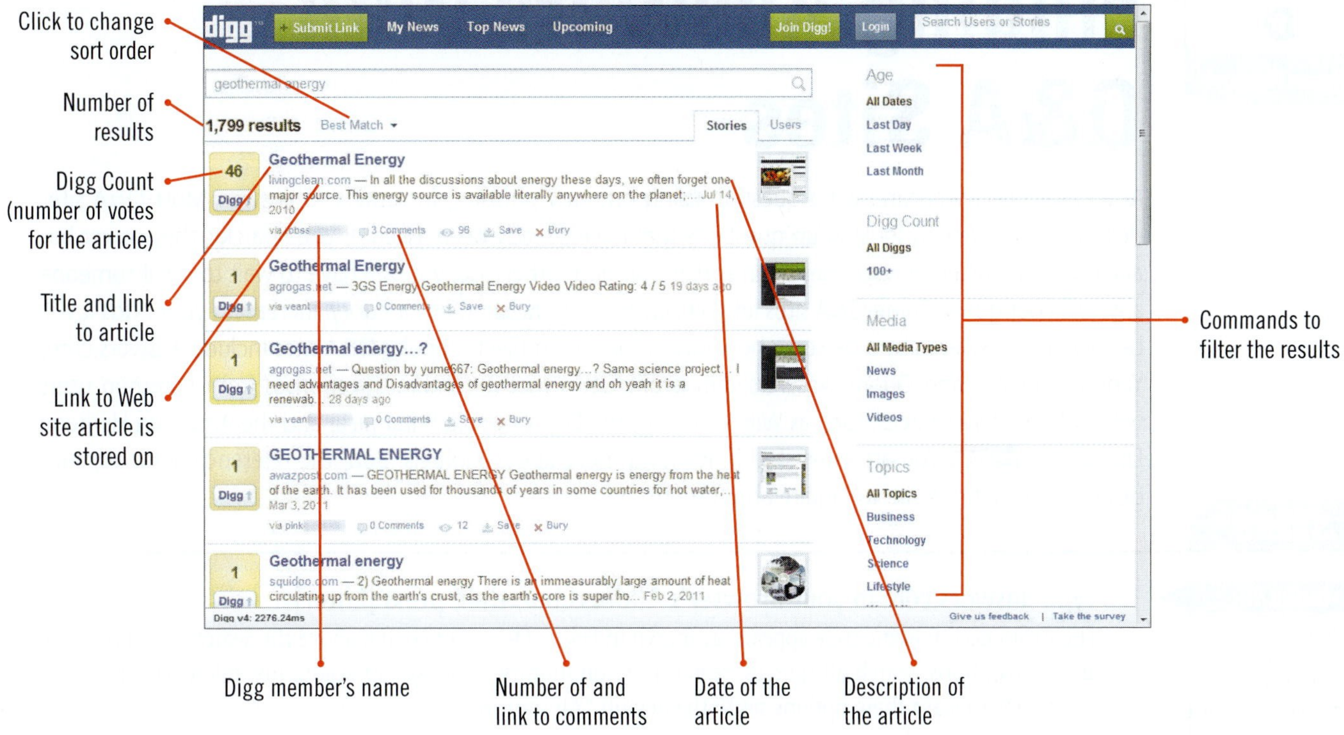

Click to change sort order

Number of results

Digg Count (number of votes for the article)

Title and link to article

Link to Web site article is stored on

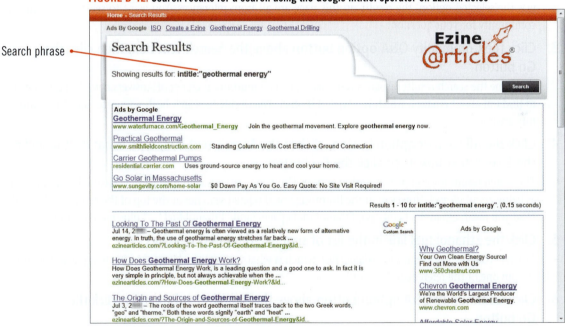

Commands to filter the results

Digg member's name

Number of and link to comments

Date of the article

Description of the article

FIGURE D-12: Search results for a search using the Google intitle: operator on EzineArticles

Search phrase

Internet Research

Searching the Social Web

Finding Answers with Q&A Sites

At a Q&A site, users can post a question using ordinary phrasing for others to answer. Most Q&A sites deliver fast answers by looking up questions that have already been asked. If you're lucky, the answer has already been posted in responses to an earlier question; otherwise, you will have to wait to see if someone answers your query. Some Q&A sites let you classify your question by category, increasing your odds it will be seen and answered by a person who knows about the subject. Popular Q&A sites include Answers.com, Yahoo! Answers, and Quora. Answers.com is unique in that it combines responses from common users with authoritative sources, such as Wikipedia.org, the Encyclopedia Britannica, and the American Heritage Dictionary.  You are interested in learning more about biofuels. Bob, the reference librarian, suggests you use a Q&A site to inquire about them.

STEPS

QUICK TIP
Some article directories specialize in publishing how-to information that can be useful for answering your questions; one of the most popular is eHow.com.

1. **Type answers.com in your browser's Address bar, then press [Enter]**

   The Answers.com home page appears, as shown in Figure D-13. Notice that above the Search text box, there are three options: search all sources, search just community responses, or search just references. For now, you decide to leave these options set to the default "All sources."

2. **Click in the Search text box, type What is biofuel?, then click the Go button**

   The search results for your question appear, similar to those shown in Figure D-14. Although "All sources" was the selected option, the results on this page are all from references. You want to see results from the community for your question.

TROUBLE
If your Search text box contains *biofuel*, retype the search question from Step 2.

3. **Click the Community Q&A option button above the Search text box, then click the Go button**

   This time the search results display a response from a community member of Answers.com. Next, you want to find out about ethanol, which is a type of biofuel. You decide to search both references and the community answers.

4. **Click the All sources option button, click in the Search text box, type What is ethanol? in the Search text box, then click the Go button**

   The search results for your new question appear. This time Answers.com mistakenly classified your question as being about *alcohol*. However, in the list of suggested related searches at the top of the results, it does ask, "Did you mean ethanol (chemistry), Ethanol (data page), and "Ethanol fuel"..." plus more options.

TROUBLE
If you don't see the list of suggested related searches, click the Go button again.

5. **Click the Ethanol fuel link in the list of suggested related searches**

   Answers.com displays results for *Ethanol fuel*, which is what you were looking for in the first place. The result is from one of the references, Wikipedia.

TROUBLE
If your Search text box contains *ethanol*, retype the search question from Step 4.

6. **Click Community Q&A option button above the Search text box, then click the Go button**

   The search results display responses to various questions about ethanol fuel from community members of Answers.com. You decide that this Q&A site provides valuable information.

FIGURE D-13: Answers.com home page

Search text box

Category question appears in

Questions most recently answered

Questions most recently asked

FIGURE D-14: Search results from All sources for *What is biofuel?* on Answers.com

Click to limit the results to results from the reference library

Click to limit the results to responses from community members

Click to return results from community members and the reference library

Sponsored result

Suggested related searches

Sponsored result

Result from reference library

Understanding a Wiki

Wikis, like a Q&A site, draw on the power of the masses to provide information. The largest, most popular one is Wikipedia. In addition, there are wiki sites, such as Wikia, which let people collaboratively build their own wikis, as well as wiki server software packages. Enterprises and academics were earlier adopters of wikis. Adobe Systems, Amazon, Intel, and Microsoft are increasingly using wikis internally for collaborative project management and information sharing. A few corporations have ventured into attempting collaboratively built customer support systems, without much success. Academic wikis include nLab for math and physics and OpenWetWare for biology.

Using Social Media Search Engines

Because social media search engines let you find information from multiple social media sites simultaneously, they can save you quite a bit of time. Table D-3 lists and describes some of the more popular social media search engines. These tools vary widely in the number and type of social media platforms they search. In addition, social media search engines differ in the control they provide over limiting and sorting search results. After searching the various social media platforms, you have become overwhelmed with the massive number of places to look on the Social Web. Bob, the reference librarian, suggests using social media search engines to find information on multiple social media sites simultaneously. You decide to search for information about wind energy companies.

STEPS

1. **Type samepoint.com in your browser's Address bar, then press [Enter]**

   The Samepoint home page appears. See Figure D-15.

2. **Click in the Search text box, type wind energy company, then click the Go button**

   A page with search results appears, as shown in Figure D-16. Note that the search results show the page title, with a brief description beneath each one, as well as the source of the page. Since many companies today have profiles on social networks such as LinkedIn, you decide to limit this search. To do this, you can click one of the tabs above the results, or you can click the Social Networks button in the row of buttons at the top of the page.

3. **Click the LinkedIn tab above the results**

   After a few moments, your search results change to display only those from LinkedIn. The title of each result is a person, company name, or group name on LinkedIn. In addition, the page displays the total number of mentions within major business social networks.

   > **TROUBLE**
   > To view details about the company or group, you might need to log in to LinkedIn.

4. **Scroll through the search results, then click a link to a company that appears relevant to your needs**

   After the company's LinkedIn page appears in your browser window, investigate exactly what services they provide, determine how long the business or group has been in existence, and attempt to find a list of their clients or members as a means to evaluate the qualifications of the companies. Next, you decide to search general-purpose social networks.

5. **Click your browser's Back button to return to the results page on Samepoint, then click the Social Networks button in the row of buttons at the top of the page**

   After a few moments, your search results show results from sites, such as Bebo, Friendster, and Tagged. The first tab, Ning, is selected by default.

6. **Scroll through the search results, then click a link that appears relevant to your needs**

7. **Look over the page, then click your browser Back button**

   You can click another tab to see the results from a different social network.

8. **Click the Bebo tab, then examine the list of results**

   Notice that the results on this tab contain different companies than those listed on the Ning tab.

FIGURE D-15: Samepoint home page

Search text box

FIGURE D-16: Search results for *wind energy companies* on Samepoint

Click a tab to filter the results

Click a tab to sort the results by the social media site on the tab label

Title and link to result

Date result page was last modified

Description of result

Click to limit the results to LinkedIn

TABLE D-3: Social media search engines

search engine	URL	search features
SocialMention	socialmention.com	• Search over 80 social media sites • Specify which social media categories
Samepoint	www.samepoint.com	• Search a wide variety of social media sites • Filter results by social media platform
Topsy	topsy.com	• Use Boolean commands • Restrict search to a date range
Whos Talkin	whostalkin.com	• Search over 60 social media sites • Provides a gadget to use from Google
48ers	48ers.com	• Searches Twitter, Facebook, Google Buzz, Digg, and Delicious • Provides links to current trends on social media sites

Practice

SAM

Concepts Review

For current SAM information, including versions and content details, visit SAM Central (http://www.cengage.com/samcentral). If you have a SAM user profile, you may have access to hands-on instruction, practice, and assessment of the skills covered in this unit. Since various versions of SAM are supported throughout the life of this text, check with your instructor for the correct instructions and URL/Web site for accessing assignments.

Match each component of the Digg page shown in Figure D-17 to an item in the list.

FIGURE D-17

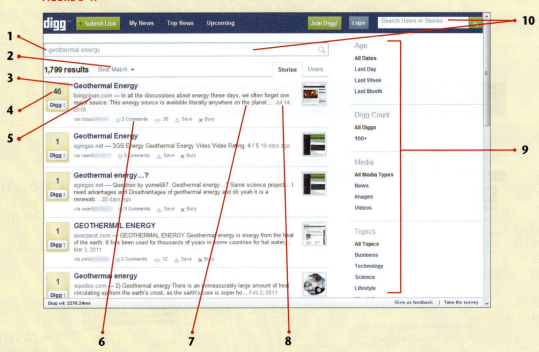

a. Digg Count
b. Commands to filter the results
c. Site on which article is posted
d. Search phrase

e. Click to change the sort order
f. Search text boxes
g. Title and link to article

h. Article description
i. Article date
j. Link to comments

Match each term with the statement that best describes it.

11. **Searching the Social Web**
12. **Microblog**
13. **Social media search engine**
14. **Blog**
15. **Social news site**
16. **Photo sharing site**
17. **Social network**

a. Enables users to post entries, such as commentaries and other material, including graphics or video

b. Allows users to upload images for public or private sharing

c. Enables you to locate information using social media platforms

d. A tool that lets you find information, usually in real time, from multiple social media sites simultaneously

e. A form of blogging, with the main difference being significant limits on the length of posts

f. Allows users to submit links to news stories or other Web pages by topic, and vote and comment on them

g. Enables people to easily establish relationships and virtual communities by sharing personal profiles, participating in groups, and exchanging private and public messages

Select the best answer from the list of choices.

18. Which of the following is not a social media platform?
   a. Social networks
   b. Blogs
   c. TV news
   d. Q&A sites

19. The most visited social media site is:
   a. Facebook.
   b. MySpace.
   c. Twitter.
   d. YouTube.

20. LinkedIn is a favorite social network for:
   a. rock bands.
   b. businesses.
   c. photographers.
   d. video enthusiasts.

21. You can use blog search engines to quickly search:
   a. discussion groups.
   b. Twitter.
   c. all social networks.
   d. the blogosphere.

22. Twitter users group topics together using:
   a. hashtags.
   b. search operators.
   c. tweets.
   d. @search.

23. To find an individual's collection of video clips on YouTube, you would check the person's YouTube:
   a. email address.
   b. blog.
   c. channel.
   d. tags.

24. Articles found in an article directory are:
   a. lengthy.
   b. original.
   c. dense with keywords.
   d. written by a professional author.

25. Social media search engines find information on multiple social media sites:
   a. sequentially.
   b. in succession.
   c. serially.
   d. simultaneously.

Skills Review

1. Identify social media platforms.
   a. Describe social networks.
   b. Explain how blogs work.
   c. Describe the main differences between blogs and microblogs.
   d. Describe what video and photo sharing sites do.
   e. Explain the difference between social news sites and article directories.
   f. Explain how Q&A sites work.

2. Understand social media searches.
   a. Explain why it can be a good idea to become a member of a site on the Social Web.
   b. Explain how tags are used on social media platforms.
   c. Describe what a social media search engine does.
   d. Describe how a blog search engine works.

3. Search social networks.
   a. Go to **linkedin.com**, then log into your profile.
   b. Use the LinkedIn Advanced People Search page to find employees that currently work for the company **First Solar**. If requested by your instructor, print or save this page of results.
   c. Explore the search results to find a person with expertise in solar energy.

Skills Review (continued)

4. **Navigate the blogosphere.**

   a. Go to **technorati.com**.

   b. Use Technorati's search tools to locate blogs about **geothermal energy**. If requested by your instructor, print or save this page of results.

   c. Examine the results, go to a blog with an authority rating over 300, if possible, and then examine several posts at the blog to judge the expertise of the owner.

   d. Return to your Technorati search results, and then refine the search to filter the results to those that fit in the Technology category. If requested by your instructor, print or save this page of results.

   e. Find another blog whose owner likely has expertise in geothermal energy and examine it.

5. **Scan microblogs.**

   a. Go to **twitter.com**.

   b. Search for tweets about **biomass energy**. If requested by your instructor, print or save this page of results.

   c. Examine the search results for messages with worthwhile information.

   d. Search for tweets tagged with the hashtag **#biomass**. If requested by your instructor, print or save this page of results.

   e. Search for tweets that mention the biomass company **wood2energy**, a company that posts tweets. If requested by your instructor, print or save this page of results.

   f. Construct a complex query to find tweets posted by people that live near **Portland, OR**, and mention **biomass**. If requested by your instructor, print or save this page of results.

6. **Search video and photo sharing sites.**

   a. Go to **youtube.com**.

   b. Search for a video that explains **how solar energy works**. If requested by your instructor, print or save this page of results.

   c. Select one of the results, then watch that video.

   d. Construct a complex query to find additional videos on this topic, this time using the synonyms **sun** and **photoelectric** instead of the term *solar*.

   e. Sort the results by View count. If requested by your instructor, print or save this page of results.

   f. Watch the video that has been viewed the most often.

   g. Go to **flickr.com**.

   h. Use Flickr's Advanced Search page to search for any type of graphic featuring **solar energy**. If requested by your instructor, print or save this page of results.

   i. Display the photographer's photostream. If requested by your instructor, print or save this page of results.

7. **Search social news sites and article directories.**

   a. Go to **digg.com**.

   b. Search for news articles about **hydroelectric energy**.

   c. Sort the articles from the most popular to the least. If requested by your instructor, print or save this page of results.

   d. Go to **ezinearticles.com**.

   e. Find all the articles at EzineArticles with **"hydroelectric energy"** in their titles. If requested by your instructor, print or save this page of results.

   f. Read one of the articles that looks interesting.

8. **Find answers with Q&A sites.**

   a. Go to **answers.com**.

   b. Search for information about **ocean thermal energy** using all sources available at Answers.com. If requested by your instructor, print or save this page of results.

   c. Examine the sources and quality of the information returned by Answers.com.

   d. Ask just the Q&A Community **How does ocean thermal energy work?**

   e. Read the answer. If requested by your instructor, print or save this page of results.

Skills Review (continued)

9. Use social media search engines.

a. Go to **samepoint.com**.

b. Search for a **solar energy company**, and then filter the results to display only those from Facebook. If requested by your instructor, print or save this page of results.

c. Explore a few of the search results to locate companies that specialize in windmill energy.

d. Return to the Samepoint search results, then filter the results to display only those results posted by a government agency. If requested by your instructor, print or save this page of results displayed on the default tab of All Gov.

e. Examine several of the new search results.

Independent Challenge 1

You have heard Google is a great place to work. You want to check out some of the people that work there using a social network.

a. Go to **linkedin.com**, and then log into your profile.

b. Find people who currently work at Google. If requested by your instructor, print or save this page of results.

c. Explore several of the Google employee pages, paying special attention to their qualifications.

d. Filter the search to include only those people that include the keyword **manager**. If requested by your instructor, print or save this page of results.

Advanced Challenge Exercise

- Click the Jobs option in the LinkedIn header bar, click Find Jobs, and then search for **web designer** positions.
- Use the Advanced Jobs Search form to look for positions with the job title **web designer** at **Google** company, and then explore the results.
- Narrow the results to within 50 miles of your zip code, and then explore the results. (If no results were returned from the previous search at Google, first remove *Google* from the Company text box.) If requested by your instructor, print or save this page of results.

e. If you have a Facebook account, go to **facebook.com**, then search Facebook to find Google's Facebook page. If requested by your instructor, print or save this page of results.

f. If you do not have a Facebook account, go to **google.com**, type **google site:facebook.com** to use the site operator to search for the text *Google* on Facebook. If requested by your instructor, print or save this page of results. Click the link to Google's Facebook page, which is probably the first result.

g. Examine the page, and pay attention to the other Google pages listed under "Likes." Consider visiting these pages to find out more about the company.

Independent Challenge 2

You work in advertising, and your company is considering expanding to social media marketing. You have heard about this topic and want to learn more.

a. Go to **icerocket.com**.

b. Use the Search text box to conduct a search about **social media marketing**. If requested by your instructor, print or save this page of results.

c. Explore several of the top blogs about the topic, and read a few relevant posts.

d. Go to **google.com**, click the More link at the top, and then click Blogs to open the Google blogs page. (If you don't see those links, go to **blogsearch.google.com**.)

e. Conduct a search for blogs about **social media marketing**. If requested by your instructor, print or save this page of results.

f. Explore several of the top blogs about the topic, and read a few relevant posts.

g. Click the Past 24 hours link on the left to filter the results to posts during that time period. If requested by your instructor, print or save this page of results.

Advanced Challenge Exercise

- Use the tilde (~) Google advanced operator in front of the key term *marketing* to find a broader list of blogs about *social media marketing*, as it will search for blogs that use a synonym in place of *marketing*. If requested by your instructor, print or save this page of results.

- Explore the search results of top blogs on this topic, and then subscribe to the RSS feed of the most interesting blog you find. If requested by your instructor, print or save this page of results. (After you finish this exercises, delete the feed; if you are using Internet Explorer, open the Favorites panel, click Feeds, right-click the feed you added, and then click Delete.)

- Scroll to the bottom of the page, and then click the link to create an email alert for *social media ~marketing*, fill in your email address on the page that appears, and then click Create Alert. Check your email for the first message. If requested by your instructor, print or save this email.

Independent Challenge 3

You want to take a vacation, but you have never been outside the country. You want to see what people are saying about traveling abroad.

a. Go to **twitter.com**.

b. Conduct a search using the query **travelling abroard**. If requested by your instructor, print or save this page of results.

c. Scroll down the list of results, and then click one that seems to have general information about travelling abroard.

d. Read the information, and then return to your Twitter search results.

e. Conduct a search using the query **travel tips** with a hashtag in front of each term. If requested by your instructor, print or save this page of results.

f. Scroll down the list of results, and then read several of the tips.

g. Return to your Twitter search results, and then search for tweets with tips about travelling to Mexico. If requested by your instructor, print or save this page of results.

h. Scroll down the list of results, and then read several of the messages.

Real Life Independent Challenge

Job interviews have become highly competitive, with tougher questions, better-trained interviewers, and well-prepared applicants. Your chances of performing well in a job interview can be improved with practice and insightful tips. Use a video sharing service to find a job training video, with advice on how to practice for a job interview.

a. Go to **youtube.com**.

b. Conduct a search using the query **how practice "job interview"**. If requested by your instructor, print or save this page of results.

c. Scroll down the list of videos on the results page, and then watch one that looks useful.

d. Conduct another search for **video resume tips**. If requested by your instructor, print or save this page of results.

e. Scroll down the list of results, and then watch one that provides tips on creating a video resume.

f. Go to **ezinearticles.com**.

g. Conduct a search for an article using the same query that you used initially on youtube.com (**how practice "job interview"**). If requested by your instructor, print or save this page of results.

h. Scroll down the list of articles on the results page, and then read one that appears worthwhile.

i. Conduct another search using the query **when to use video resume**. If requested by your instructor, print or save this page of results.

j. Scroll down the list of results, and then read a few of the articles.

Visual Workshop

Use Flickr.com to find the photograph shown in Figure D-18. This photograph shows the Fredericksborg Castle in Copenhagen, Denmark. If requested by your instructor, print or save the page on the photo sharing site on which this photo is displayed.

FIGURE D-18

Internet Research Sites Appendix

Site	URL
Article Directories	
ArticlesBase.com	www.articlesbase.com
eHow	www.ehow.com
EzineArticles	www.ezinearticles.com
GoArticles.com	www.goarticles.com
Knol	www.knol.google.com
Blog Sites	
Blogger	www.blogger.com
Tumblr	www.tumblr.com
WordPress	www.wordpress.com
Blog Search Engine	
BlogPulse	www.blogpulse.com
Google Blog Search	www.blogsearch.google.com
IceRocket	www.icerocket.com
Technorati	www.technorati.com
Discussion Boards	
Boardreader	www.boardreader.com
BoardTracker	www.boardtracker.com
Google Groups	www.groups.google.com
Yahoo! Groups	www.groups.yahoo.com
Flickr Search Engines	
FlickrBabel	www.flickrbabel.com
FlickrStorm	www.zoo-m.com/flickr-storm
liteFlick.com	www.liteflick.com
Tag Galaxy	www.taggalaxy.de
Government Portals	
Australian Government	www.australia.gov.au
Directgov	www.direct.gov.uk
FedWorld	www.fedworld.gov
Government of Canada	www.canada.gc.ca
U.S. Government Printing Office (GPO)	www.gpo.gov
GPO Access	www.gpoaccess.gov
National Technical Information Service (NTIS)	www.ntis.gov
University of Michigan Government Documents Center	www.lib.umich.edu/government-documents-center
USA.gov	www.usa.gov
U.S. Census Bureau	www.census.gov
Keyword Tool	
Google AdWords Keyword Tool	www.adwords.google.com
Mapping Web Sites	
Bing Maps	www.bing.com/maps
Google Maps	www.maps.google.com
Maps on Us	www.mapsonus.com

Site	URL
MapQuest	www.mapquest.com
MapQuest	www.mapquest.co.uk
MapQuest (Deutschland)	www.mapquest.de
MapQuest (France)	www.mapquest.fr
Rand McNally Travel Store	http://maps.randmcnally.com
Streetmap	www.streetmap.co.uk
Yahoo! Maps	www.maps.yahoo.com
Metasearch Engines	
Dogpile	www.dogpile.com
MetaCrawler	www.metacrawler.com
Startpage	www.startpage.com
WebCrawler	www.webcrawler.com
Yippy	www.yippy.com
Microblogs	
FriendFeed	www.friendfeed.com
Google Buzz	www.google.com/buzz
Jaiku	www.jaiku.com
Plurk	www.plurk.com
Tumblr	www.tumblr.com
Twitter	www.twitter.com
News Aggregators	
Google News	www.news.google.com
Online Reference Sources	
FILExt	www.filext.com
Infoplease	www.infoplease.com
Internet Tutorials	www.internettutorials.net
ipl2	www.ipl2.org
Netiquette Home Page	www.albion.com/netiquette
Webopedia	www.webopedia.com
Living Internet	www.livinginternet.com
Periodical Databases	
MagPortal	www.magportal.com
Periodicals	
First Monday	www.firstmonday.org
Harvard Educational Review	www.hepg.org/her
Journal of Accountancy	www.journalofaccountancy.com
People Magazine	www.people.com
Salon	www.salon.com
The New York Times	www.nytimes.com
The Times	www.thetimes.co.uk
Photo Sharing Sites	
Flickr	www.flickr.com
Photobucket	www.photobucket.com
Portals	
America Online	www.aol.com
MSN	www.msn.com

Site	URL
Q&A Sites	
Answers.com	www.answers.com
Quora	www.quora.com
Yahoo! Answers	www.answers.yahoo.com
RSS Readers	
Google Reader	www.google.com/reader
RSSOwl	www.rssowl.org
Sage	www.sagerss.com
Search Engine Guides	
Search Engine Showdown	www.searchengineshowdown.com
Search Engine Watch	www.searchenginewatch.com
Search Engines	
Bing	www.bing.com
Google	www.google.com
Yahoo!	www.yahoo.com
Search Toolbars	
Google Toolbar	www.toolbar.google.com
MSN Toolbar	http://toolbar.discoverbing.com/toolbar
Yahoo! Toolbar	www.toolbar.yahoo.com
Social Bookmarking Sites	
BlinkList	www.blinklist.com
Delicious	www.delicious.com
MyLinkVault	www.mylinkvault.com
Sphinn	www.sphinn.com
Techmeme	www.techmeme.com
Social Media Search Engines	
48ers	www.48ers.com
Samepoint	www.samepoint.com
Social Mention	www.socialmention.com
Topsy	www.topsy.com
Whos Talkin	www.whostalkin.com
Social Networks	
Bebo	www.bebo.com
Facebook	www.facebook.com
Friendster	www.friendster.com
Google+ project	www.plus.google.com
Google Buzz	www.google.com/buzz
Hi5	www.hi5.com
LinkedIn	www.linkedin.com
MySpace	www.myspace.com
Ning	www.ning.com
Orkut	www.orkut.com
Tagged	www.tagged.com
Social News Sites	
Digg	www.digg.com
Reddit	www.reddit.com
StumbleUpon	www.stumbleupon.com

Site	URL
Specialized Databases	
EBSCOhost	http://search.ebscohost.com
InfoTrac	www.infotrac.galegroup.com
ProQuest	www.proquest.com
Specialized Search Engines	
EnviroLink Network	www.envirolink.org
Scirus	www.scirus.com
Subject Guides	
EERE	www.eere.energy.gov
INFOMINE	http://infomine.ucr.edu
ipl2	www.ipl2.org
Open Directory Project	www.dmoz.org
Scout Archives	www.scout.wisc.edu/Archives
WWW Virtual Library	www.vlib.org
Useful Sites	
American Heritage Dictionary	www.dictionary.com
APA Style	www.apastyle.org
Creative Commons	www.creativecommons.org
Encyclopedia Britannica	www.britannica.com
MLA Style	www.mla.org/style
Video Sharing Sites	
YouTube	www.youtube.com
White & Yellow Pages	
411Locate	www.411locate.com
AnyWho.com	www.anywho.com
Canada411	www.canada411.ca
EUROPAGES	www.europages.com
Scoot	www.scoot.co.uk
Superpages	www.superpages.com
Switchboard.com	www.switchboard.com
Golden Pages (Ireland)	www.goldenpages.ie
ukphonebook.com	www.ukphonebook.com
WhitePages	www.whitepages.com
Yell	www.yell.com
YellowPages.ca (Canada)	www.yellowpages.ca
Yellow Pages (Australia)	www.yellowpages.com.au
YP.com	www.yp.com
Wiki Sites	
nLab	www.ncatlab.org
OpenWetWare	www.openwetware.org
Wikipedia	www.wikipedia.org

Glossary

Algorithm A mathematical formula used by a search engine to rank each Web site returned in search results according to the terms used in the search query.

AND A Boolean operator that when used to connect keywords in a search query requires that each keyword connected by it must be on a Web page for that Web page to be included in the results.

Annotation In a subject guide, a summary or review of a Web page, usually written by experts, such as professionals, academics in the field, or librarians.

Article directory A Web site that publishes articles that must be approved first.

Blog A Web site on which people post commentaries and invite comments from viewers.

Blogosphere All blog content and the interconnections that form a social network.

Boolean algebra *See* Boolean logic.

Boolean logic The field of mathematics that defines how Boolean operators manipulate large sets of data by connecting keywords with Boolean operators. *Also called* Boolean algebra.

Boolean operators Command words such as AND, OR, and AND NOT that narrow, expand, or restrict a search based on Boolean logic.

Cached page A copy of a Web page that resides on a search engine's computer.

Channel The home page of a YouTube account holder.

Citation format A style guide that standardizes references to resources like books, magazine articles, and Web pages; common formats are those by MLA (Modern Language Association) and APA (American Psychological Association).

Complex search query A search query that uses Boolean operators to define the relationships between keywords and phrases in a way that search tools can interpret.

Deep Web The part of the Web inaccessible to search engine spiders and consisting primarily of information housed in databases. *Also called* invisible Web.

Default operator The Boolean operator that a search engine automatically uses in a query, whether typed as part of the query or not. Most search engines default to the AND operator, although a few default to the OR operator.

Discussion board A Web site that allows people to exchange message asynchronously.

Discussion group A collection of related topics on a discussion board.

Discussion forum *See* discussion group.

Distributed subject guide A subject guide created by a variety of editors working somewhat independently and usually stored on numerous computers located around the country or the world.

Drill down To click through subject headings (or topics or categories) to reach relevant links.

Dynamically generated Web page A Web page generated by a database in response to a specific query.

Evaluative criteria Standards used to determine if a Web site is appropriate for your needs, including considerations of organization, authority, objectivity, accuracy, scope, and currency.

Hierarchy A ranked order.

Hashtag A word in a tweet that the author identifies by typing the pound, or hash, sign operator (#) before the word to create topical categories that others can search for.

Internet A vast global network of interconnected networks.

Internet directory *See* Subject guide.

Internet search tool A service that helps locate information on the Web, including search engines, metasearch engines, subject guides, specialized search engines, and social media search engines.

Intersection The place where two sets overlap in a Venn diagram.

Invisible Web *See* deep Web.

Keyword An important word that describes a major concept of your search topic.

Keyword density The percentage of words in articles on article directories that are words that people would tend to use to search for information about the topic in the article.

Keyword generator A tool that produces related keywords by using synonyms, plurals, misspellings, and other grammatical inflections.

Metasearch engine A search tool that searches the indexes of multiple search engines simultaneously.

Microblog A blog that significantly limits the length of posts.

Mnemonic Assisting or aiding memory.

NOT A Boolean operator that when used to connect keywords in a search query requires that each keyword connected by it must *not* be on a Web page for that Web page to be included in the results.

News aggregator A Web site that collects headlines from news sources and lists them as links.

Online reference source A digital version of an almanac, dictionary, encyclopedia, and other similar resources available on the Internet.

OR A Boolean operator that when used to connect keywords in a search query requires that at least one of the keywords connected by it appears on a Web page for that Web page to be included in the results.

Periodical database A specialized database that usually requires a paid subscription, is available only at libraries, and contains the full text of articles from periodicals, such as newspapers, magazines, and journals.

Photo sharing site A Web site on which people upload and share photos.

Photostream The home page of the account holder on Flickr.

Phrase search To force a search tool to search only for pages containing two or more words together in a certain order; typically, quotation marks are used around the words to indicate that they should be searched as a phrase.

Portal A large Web gateway providing access to huge amounts of information via search engines, news, shopping, email, chat, and more. *See also* vortal.

Post (n.) A published blog entry.

Post (v.) To publish a blog entry or comment.

Q&A site *See* question-and-answer site.

Query *See* search query.

Question-and-answer (Q&A) site A social search tool that lets you pose a question and receive answers from anyone willing to reply.

RSS (Really Simple Syndication) A protocol that gives you the ability to selectively subscribe to automatic updates from a wide variety of social media platforms.

RSS reader Software that allows you to receive and view RSS feeds.

Search engine A search tool, usually indexed by spiders, that locates Web pages containing the keywords entered in a search form.

Search engine optimization (SEO) The process of fine-tuning a Web site so that it ranks at the top of search engine results.

Search query Keywords, phrases, and Boolean operators entered into a search form that the search tool uses to search its index.

Search result A Web page returned by a search tool in response to a search.

Set A collection of objects; in a Venn diagram, sets are represented by circles.

Social bookmarking site A site on which people store and describe their favorite Web pages with descriptors (tags), allowing you to search for popular content.

Social media search engine A search tool that searches only the Social Web.

Social media platform How social media is presented on the Web, including social networks, blogs, microblogs, video and photo sharing sites, social news sites, article directories, Q&A sites, bookmarking sites, news aggregators, and wiki sites.

Social media site A Web site that contains content from a type of social media platform.

Social network An online community where people form relationships based on everything from friendship and workplace affiliations to common interests and shared beliefs.

Social news site A Web site that allows users to submit news stories or other Web pages and vote on news stories posted by others.

Social Web The collection of social media sites on the Web.

Specialized search engine A search engine that limits the Web pages it indexes by subject.

Spider A computer program that scans, or crawls the Web to index Web pages without making judgments regarding the value of indexing a page, as human indexers do.

Stop word A common word, such as *a, and, the, for,* or *of,* that is not normally searched by search tools.

Subject directory *See* Subject guide.

Subject guide A search tool that hierarchically arranges links to Web pages. The links are evaluated and annotated by people, usually subject specialists or librarians, rather than spiders. *Also called* Internet directory, subject directory, or subject tree.

Subject tree *See* Subject guide.

Surface Web *See* visible Web.

Synonym A word that has a similar meaning to another word.

Syntax The rules of a language, like grammar, that standardize usage.

Tag A key word that identifies the contents of blog and microblog posts, videos, photos, articles, and questions on Q&A sites to give search engines another key word to index.

Tag cloud A presentation of tags in which the font size of the text indicates how often the tag is used.

Thread A subtopic in a discussion group, arranged In chronological order.

Trending search A current, popular search phrase on the Internet.

Union The combination of two sets in a Venn diagram.

Venn diagram A drawing, typically comprised of intersecting circles, used to illustrate Boolean logic or searches using Boolean operators.

Video sharing site A Web site on which people upload and share videos.

Visible Web The portion of the Web that is indexed by search engine spiders; also might refer to parts of the Web that, although not crawled by spiders, are indexed by subject guides. *Also called* surface Web.

Vortal Short for vertical portal, a portal that focuses on only one topic or industry.

World Wide Web An enormous repository of information stored on millions of computers all over the world.

Web log *See* blog.

Wiki Server software that lets anyone create and modify Web page content.

Index